# THE IRISH GRANNY'S
## *pocket*
# FARMHOUSE
# KITCHEN

Gill Books
Hume Avenue, Park West, Dublin 12

www.gillbooks.ie

Gill Books is an imprint of M.H. Gill & Co.

Copyright © Teapot Press Ltd 2018

ISBN: 978-0-7171-7943-5

This book was created and produced by Teapot Press Ltd

Recipes compiled by Fiona Biggs
Designed by Tony Potter
Picture research and photography by Ben Potter
Home economics by
Christine Potter, Imogen Tyler & Anne Wright

Printed in Europe

This book is typeset in Garamond and Dax

A CIP catalogue record for this book is available
from the British Library.

5 4 3 2

# The Irish Granny's
*pocket*
# FARMHOUSE
# KITCHEN

Fiona Biggs

Gill Books

# Contents

### From the Bake Oven

### Preserves

### From the Stillroom

### Let's Celebrate!

# Introduction

The Irish kitchen is the heart of the home, nowhere more so than in the farmhouses of rural Ireland. The old farmhouse recipes still form the basis of the modern Irish culinary repertoire, utilising good and wholesome ingredients cooked from scratch.

Farmhouse meals were traditionally served in large portions, designed to keep hungry farm workers going throughout the long day of physical work. Main dishes were usually accompanied a mound of boiled or mashed potatoes, and the butter, eggs, cream and cheese produced on the farm all had a starring role to play in the everyday recipes.

The kitchen garden was the domain of the women of the house, who were responsible for producing all the vegetables and soft fruit consumed the household. Spring and summer vegetables were eaten in abundance during their short seasons and preserved for use in the leaner winter months, when cabbages, cauliflowers and root vegetables were the only produce from the kitchen garden. Soft fruits were eaten fresh, incorporated in cold summer desserts and made into luscious jams that could be eaten throughout the year. Even if there was no orchard, there were usually a few apple and plum trees in the garden, producing enough fruit for plenty of delicious tarts and pies.

Even in those farmhouses that were far from the sea fish and seafood formed the basis of the main meal once a week, and more frequently during Lent. The Irish people worked their way around the Catholic Church restriction on meat-eating during Lent and on Fridays turning to fish. Fish was therefore disparaged as penitential food until over-fishing inevitably enhanced its value. Coastal residents went to their local harbour to buy fish, while landlocked farmers' wives would have shopped at their local fishmonger – shellfish such as mussels and oysters were cheap and plentiful and were frequently incorporated in other dishes, even those that included meat.

Baking bread and scones was a daily occurrence – soda bread, made with buttermilk, was eaten throughout the day – at breakfast with a traditional fry-up, with the lunchtime soup or cheese, or spread with delicious home-made jam as a snack. It is the ideal bread for a busy cook – there's no proving involved, and the batter is just mixed and put in the oven. Cakes were generally hearty fruit cakes, such as porter cake, or cut-and-come-again cakes like ginger cake or Madeira cake, but the occasional indulgent afternoon tea cake was produced for Sundays – coffee and walnut cake and Victoria sponge were particular favourites.

Desserts were another infrequent treat – always on Sundays, occasionally during the week. Sunday desserts were fancier, while weekday offerings tended to be fruit pies, crumbles and steamed puddings, using fresh or preserved ingredients from the garden.

Making drinks, both alcoholic and non-alcoholic, was all part of the activity of the farm. Wine was made from a variety of ingredients, including root vegetables, berries and even dandelions. Tangy lemonades and barley waters were cool refreshing drinks in the summer. Sloes and red berries were often used to disguise the harshness of inferior spirits.

Nothing says farmhouse cooking quite like a pie, and pastry-making was a regular occurrence in the farmhouse kitchen. The recipe on page 11 will cover one pie or make one pie base. If your recipe calls for a double crust, double the quantities. The secret to good pastry is to keep the ingredients chilled and your hands cold.

# PASTRY

### INGREDIENTS

125 g/4½ oz plain flour

pinch of salt

55 g/2 oz chilled butter, diced

2–3 tbsp chilled water

### METHOD

Put the flour and salt into a large bowl and add the butter.

Rub the butter into the flour with your fingertips until coarse crumbs form.

Use a knife to stir in just enough water to bind the dough together.

Wrap the dough in clingfilm and chill in the refrigerator for 10–15 minutes before using.

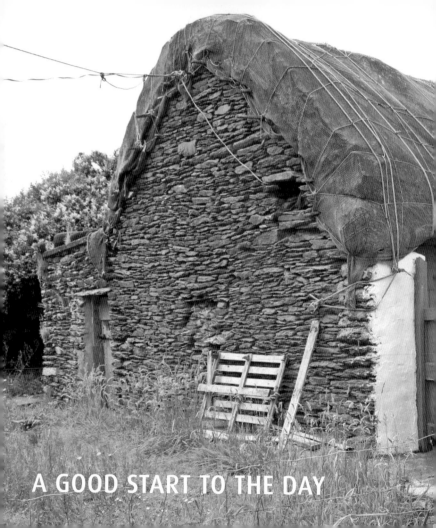

A GOOD START TO THE DAY

## INGREDIENTS

85 g/3 oz rolled oats
200 ml/7 fl oz milk
300 ml/10 fl oz water
150 g/5½ oz fresh or frozen mixed berries, such as raspberries, blueberries, blackberries and strawberries, thawed if frozen
25 g/1 oz toasted flaked almonds

# Porridge with Berries

Preparing porridge with a mixture of milk and water makes it very creamy. The nuts and berries add a luxurious touch.

## METHOD

Put the oats into a saucepan and add the milk and water. Cook over a medium heat for about 10 minutes, stirring constantly to prevent sticking, until smooth and creamy.

Divide the porridge between two bowls. Top with the berries, scatter the almonds over and serve immediately.

SERVES 2

## INGREDIENTS

1 tomato, halved
vegetable oil, for
drizzling and frying
2 pork sausages
2 back bacon rashers
1 slice white
pudding
1 slice black pudding
1 large egg
salt and freshly
ground black pepper
fresh white soda
bread (see page
172), to serve

# Full Irish Breakfast

This hearty fry, now an occasional
calorie-laden treat in Irish homes, was a
favourite with farm workers as it kept
them going until lunchtime.

## METHOD

Drizzle the tomato halves with oil and season with salt and
pepper. Place the sausages on a rack under a hot grill and cook,
turning once, for about 15 minutes until browned all over.
Add the tomatoes during the last 4 minutes of cooking.

Meanwhile, put the rashers into a dry frying pan over a high
heat and fry for 3 minutes on each side, or until cooked to your
liking.

Remove from the pan using a slotted spoon, drain on kitchen
paper and keep warm.

Add the white and black pudding slices to the pan, fry for
1–2 minutes on each side, then remove from the pan, drain
on kitchen paper and keep warm.

Heat some oil in a separate small frying pan, carefully break in
the egg and fry over a low heat until cooked to your liking.

Transfer all the cooked ingredients to a warmed plate and serve
with plenty of soda bread.

**SERVES 1**

## INGREDIENTS

1-2 large kippers
1 tsp unsalted butter
for each kipper
scrambled eggs (see
page 22), to serve

# Kippers

These are delicious served with hot buttered toast. Kippers are often fried, but baking them in water makes them succulent and a little less salty.

## METHOD

Preheat the oven to 190°C/375°F/Gas Mark 5.

Place the kippers in a roasting tin and pour over enough boiling water to cover them completely.

Bake in the preheated oven for about 8 minutes, then remove from the oven and drain well.

Transfer to warmed serving plates and top each fish with a knob of butter. Serve immediately with scrambled eggs.

SERVES 1

## INGREDIENTS

2 potatoes, coarsely grated

¼ onion, finely chopped (red onion looks attractive)

20 g/¾ oz plain flour

5 eggs

vegetable oil, for frying

salt and freshly ground black pepper

# Poached Eggs on Hashed Potatoes

## METHOD

Place the potatoes in a colander and rinse under cold running water until the water runs clear. Drain well, place in a clean tea towel and twist the towel to squeeze as much water as possible out of the potatoes.

Place the potatoes in a mixing bowl, add the onion, flour and 1 egg and mix well to combine. Season to taste with salt and pepper.

Heat some oil in a large frying pan. Place large spoonfuls of the potato mixture in the pan, flattening each pile to a thickness of about 1 cm/½ inch. Cook for about 5 minutes on each side until golden brown and cooked through.

Remove from the pan, drain on kitchen paper and keep warm.

Meanwhile, bring a large saucepan of water to the boil over a high heat, then reduce the heat until the water is simmering briskly.

Crack each of the 4 remaining eggs into a cup, one at a time, and carefully tip the eggs into the water, towards the edge of the pan. Cook for 3–4 minutes, then remove from the pan with a slotted spoon and drain on kitchen paper.

Place the hashed potatoes on serving plates, top each portion with a poached egg and serve immediately.

**SERVES 4**

## INGREDIENTS

8 large eggs
2 tbsp single cream
55 g/2 oz butter
salt and freshly
ground black pepper
hot buttered toast,
to serve
snipped fresh chives,
to garnish

# Creamy Scrambled Eggs on Toast

Eggs scrambled with cream provide a
substantial breakfast that's quick and easy
to prepare.

## METHOD

Beat the eggs with the cream in a large bowl and season to taste
with salt and pepper.

Melt the butter in a frying pan over a medium heat. Add the
eggs to the pan and cook, stirring occasionally, for about 3
minutes, until just cooked.

Remove the pan from the heat and serve the eggs immediately
on hot buttered toast, garnished with a sprinkling of chives.

SERVES 4

# EASY LUNCHES AND SNACKS

Farmland in Kerry

## INGREDIENTS

1 tbsp vegetable oil

25 g/1 oz butter

2 large leeks, roughly sliced

½ head cauliflower, roughly chopped, stem included

2 garlic cloves, finely chopped

500 ml/18 fl oz chicken or vegetable stock

125 ml/4 fl oz double cream

salt and freshly ground black pepper

chopped fresh parsley, to garnish

# Leek & Cauliflower Soup

The cauliflower adds great flavour to this soup. Add a touch of luxury with a good dollop of cream stirred in at the end.

## METHOD

Heat the oil and butter in a large saucepan over a medium heat, then add the leeks, cauliflower and garlic and sauté for 10 minutes.

Add the stock, increase the heat to high and bring to the boil. Reduce the heat to low, cover and simmer for 45 minutes.

Remove from the heat and add salt and pepper to taste. Blend the soup with a hand-held blender until smooth, then stir in the cream.

Ladle the soup into warmed bowls, garnish with parsley and serve immediately.

**SERVES 4-6**

## INGREDIENTS

1 tbsp vegetable oil
1 onion, finely chopped
1 large potato, diced
450 g/1 lb carrots, chopped
1 litre/1¾ pints chicken or vegetable stock
salt and freshly ground black pepper
fresh watercress, to garnish

# Carrot Soup

This soup is very quick to prepare. You can spice it up adding a little ground cumin or coriander or a teaspoon of whole black peppercorns with the stock.

## METHOD

Heat the oil in a large saucepan over a medium heat, add the onion and fry until softened and translucent. Stir in the potato and cook for 1 minute.

Add the carrots and stock, then increase the heat to high and bring to the boil. Reduce the heat and cook for 20 minutes, or until the carrots are soft and tender.

Remove from the heat, add salt and pepper to taste and blend with a hand-held blender until smooth. Ladle into warmed bowls, garnish with watercress and serve immediately.

**SERVES 4-6**

## INGREDIENTS

75 g/2¾ oz young
nettles

55 g/2 oz butter

25 g/1 oz porridge
oats

425 ml/ 15 fl oz
chicken or vegetable
stock

150 ml/ 5 fl oz milk

salt and freshly
ground black pepper

single cream, to
garnish

# Nettle Soup

With their reputation for cleansing the
system, nettles have been popular in Irish
kitchens for a hundreds of years. Use
young nettles for their sweeter flavour.

## METHOD

Chop the nettle leaves very finely, discarding any stalks.

Heat the butter in a large saucepan until melted. Add the oats
and cook, stirring constantly, until golden.

Remove from the heat and gradually stir in the stock. Bring to
the boil, then add the milk and bring back to the boil.

Add the nettles and cook for 5 minutes. Season to taste with salt
and pepper and ladle into warmed bowls.

Garnish with a swirl of cream and serve immediately.

**Granny's tip:** Always wear gloves when handling fresh
nettles.

**SERVES 6**

## INGREDIENTS

25 g/1 oz butter

4 back bacon rashers, chopped

4 leeks, thickly sliced

450 g/1 lb potatoes, diced

700 ml/1¼ pints vegetable stock

150 ml/5 fl oz single cream

salt and freshly ground black pepper

finely chopped fresh herbs, to garnish

# Potato & Leek Soup

Potatoes and leeks are a winning combination. The addition of bacon turns this soup into a meal in a bowl.

## METHOD

Heat the butter in a large saucepan until melted. Add the bacon and cook for 2–3 minutes until beginning to crisp.

Add the leeks to the pan and cook for 5 minutes, then add the potatoes, stock and salt and pepper to taste. Bring to the boil, then reduce the heat and simmer for 40 minutes.

Remove from the heat and blend with a hand-held blender until smooth. Stir in the cream and reheat over a low heat without boiling.

Ladle into warmed bowls, garnish with herbs and serve immediately.

**SERVES 4-6**

## INGREDIENTS

1.7 litres/3 pints
mussels, scrubbed
and debearded
1 onion, finely
chopped
1 fresh parsley sprig
150 ml/5 fl oz dry
cider
55 g/2 oz butter
2 leeks, thinly sliced
1 celery stick, finely
chopped
55 g/2 oz plain flour
1.2 litres/2 pints
milk
pinch of freshly
grated nutmeg
2 tbsp single cream
salt and freshly
ground black pepper
chopped fresh
parsley, to garnish

# Mussel Soup

Mussels are plentiful along the Irish coast
and they feature in many traditional
recipes. While white wine is the usual
ingredient in the broth, dry cider is a
delicious alternative.

## METHOD

Wash the mussels under cold running water, discarding any that
refuse to close when tapped sharply with a knife. Place them in
a large saucepan, add the onion, parsley and cider, then cover
and place over a medium heat. Cook for 3–4 minutes, shaking
frequently, until the mussels have opened.

Remove from the heat and discard any mussels that have
remained closed. Strain through a sieve, reserving the cooking
liquid. Remove the mussels from their shells and set aside.

Add the butter to the pan and heat until melted. Add the leeks
and celery and cook until softened, then stir in the flour.
Add the milk very gradually, then add the nutmeg and salt and
pepper to taste and bring to the boil. Reduce the heat and
simmer for 20 minutes. Stir in the reserved cooking liquid, the
cream and the mussels and heat over a low heat.

Ladle into warmed bowls, garnish with parsley and serve
immediately.

SERVES 4-6

## INGREDIENTS

55 g/2 oz butter

2 large onions, roughly chopped

1 ham bone with trimmings

450 g/1 lb dried peas, soaked for 3 hours and drained

1 bouquet garni of fresh herbs

1 bay leaf

2.5–3 litres/4½–5¼ pints chicken stock

salt and freshly ground pepper

chopped fresh parsley, to garnish

# Pea & Ham Soup

This soup takes several hours to cook, but the results are worth the wait and you can leave it alone once all the ingredients are in the pan. Ask your butcher for a ham bone – it adds real depth of flavour to this hearty winter soup.

## METHOD

Heat the butter in a large saucepan until melted. Add the onions and cook until softened. Add the ham bone, peas, bouquet garni and bay leaf and pour in enough stock to cover.

Bring to the boil over a low heat, then simmer for 2 hours. Remove the ham bone from the pan, trim and chop any pieces of ham and return them to the soup.

If the soup is too thick add a little water and reheat. Ladle into warmed bowls, garnish with parsley and serve immediately.

SERVES 6

## INGREDIENTS

25 g/1 oz butter
25 g/1 oz plain flour
125 ml/4 fl oz milk
1 tsp Dijon mustard
1 tsp clear honey
125 ml/4 fl oz stout
125 g/4½ oz red
Cheddar cheese,
coarsely grated
4 thick slices
wholemeal toast
halved cherry
tomatoes, to serve

# Irish Rarebit

**The inclusion of a small glass of stout in the rarebit mixture gives this snack a delicious tangy flavour.**

## METHOD

Heat the butter in a medium-sized heavy-based saucepan until melted. Quickly stir in the flour until a stiff paste forms, then cook over a low heat for 3–4 minutes to cook off the flour.

Remove from the heat and gradually add the milk to the mixture. Return to the heat and slowly bring to the boil, stirring constantly, then add the mustard, honey and stout.

Increase the heat to high and cook for 2–3 minutes, then add the cheese and cook, stirring, until the cheese has melted.

Spread the cheese mixture on the toast and place under a preheated grill until browned and bubbling.

Serve immediately with cherry tomatoes.

**SERVES 4**

## INGREDIENTS

vegetable oil, for greasing

6 large slices white bread, crusts removed

2 eggs

125 ml/4 fl oz milk

100 g/3½ oz cooked ham, roughly chopped

50 g/1¾ oz red or white Cheddar cheese, finely grated

1 tbsp finely chopped fresh flatleaf parsley

# Ham & Cheese Pies

These tasty mini pies are made with bread rather than pastry, so they're really quick to put together.

## METHOD

Preheat the oven to 180°C/350°F/Gas Mark 4. Grease 6 holes in a muffin tin.

Roll out each slice of bread with a rolling pin until very thin and lightly brush both sides with oil. Use the bread to line the holes in the muffin tin and bake in the preheated oven for 10 minutes. Remove from the oven (leave the bread cases in the tin) and reduce the oven temperature to 160°C/325°F/Gas Mark 3.

Place the eggs and milk in a mixing bowl and whisk well together. Divide the ham, cheese and parsley among the baked bread cases.

Pour the egg mixture into the bread cases, taking care not to overfill them. Return the tin to the oven and bake for a further 15–20 minutes, or until the egg is set.

Serve warm or cold.

**SERVES 6**

## INGREDIENTS

225 g/8 oz cooked cod's roe, membrane removed

85 g/3 oz fresh breadcrumbs

pinch of freshly ground nutmeg

2 tbsp finely chopped fresh parsley

juice of ½ lemon

2 eggs, separated

4 tbsp double cream

4 slices white bread, crusts removed

25 g/1 oz butter

salt and freshly ground black pepper

chopped fresh parsley, to garnish

# Cod's Roe on Toast

Cooked cod's roe is readily available in Irish fishmongers and is usually served cut into rounds and fried. This way of cooking the roes is a little more complicated, but the result is delicious.

## METHOD

Preheat the oven to 200°C/400°F/Gas Mark 6.

Put the cod's roe into a mixing bowl and mix well with the breadcrumbs, nutmeg and salt and pepper to taste.

Put the parsley, lemon juice, egg yolks and cream into a separate bowl and beat well together. Combine with the cod's roe mixture and leave to stand for 15 minutes.

Meanwhile, whisk the egg whites until they hold stiff peaks. Toast the bread and butter it on one side.

Fold the egg whites into the cod's roe mixture and spread on the slices of toast. Bake in the preheated oven for 15 minutes until the topping is golden brown and puffed up.

Garnish with parsley and serve immediately.

**SERVES 4**

## INGREDIENTS

225 g/8 oz fresh
mushrooms, sliced
600 ml/1 pint milk
55 g/2 oz butter
55 g/2 oz plain flour
salt and freshly
ground black pepper
4 slices buttered
toast, to serve

# Creamed Mushrooms on Toast

These are best prepared with field
mushrooms, but you can use chestnut
or button mushrooms if that's all that
you can find.

## METHOD

Put the mushrooms into a large saucepan, add the milk and
bring to the boil over a medium heat. Reduce the heat to low
and simmer for 10 minutes.

Meanwhile, heat the butter in a separate large saucepan until
melted. Stir in the flour until a stiff paste forms, then cook over
a low heat for about 4 minutes to cook off the flour.

Reserving the mushrooms, slowly strain the boiled milk into the
flour and butter mixture, stirring constantly, then bring to the
boil and stir until it has the consistency of a thick sauce.

Add the mushrooms, season with salt and pepper to taste and
divide the mixture equally among the toast slices.

Serve immediately.

SERVES 4

## INGREDIENTS

85 g/3 oz butter, softened

1 shallot, finely chopped

225 g/8 oz trimmed chicken livers

1 tbsp brandy

salt and freshly ground black pepper

fresh white soda bread (see page 174) and butter, to serve

# Chicken Liver Pâté

Chicken livers were a by-product of the farmyard and the occasional addition of a smooth pâté to the menu injected a little luxury into an otherwise hearty cooking repertoire.

## METHOD

Heat 25 g/1 oz of the butter in a frying pan over a medium heat until melted, then add the shallot and cook until softened and translucent. Season to taste with salt and pepper.

Increase the heat to high, add the chicken livers and cook for 2–3 minutes on each side, stirring constantly, until cooked through.

Remove from the heat and transfer the mixture to a blender or food processer and process for up to 1 minute. Add the remaining butter with the brandy and process until smooth.

Divide the mixture among four ramekins and chill in the refrigerator for at least 1 hour. Serve with bread and butter.

SERVES 4

## INGREDIENTS

225 g/8 oz cold mashed potatoes

25 g/1 oz butter, melted, plus extra for frying

55 g/2 oz red or white Cheddar cheese, coarsely grated

50 g/1¾ oz plain flour, plus extra for dusting

freshly ground black pepper

# Cheesy Potato Cakes

Potato cakes are far the best way to use up leftover mashed potatoes. This version includes Cheddar cheese, which adds extra flavour and texture.

## METHOD

Put the potatoes into a mixing bowl, add the melted butter and cheese and mix well to combine.

Add the flour with pepper to taste and work into the potatoes until a stiff dough forms.

Roll out the dough on a floured work surface to a thickness of about 1 cm/½ inch. Use a cup or a glass to cut into rounds.

Melt some butter in a large, heavy-based frying pan, add the potato cakes, in batches if necessary, and cook for 3 minutes on each side until crisp and golden.

Serve immediately.

**Granny's tip:** The secret to a good potato cake is not to include too much flour – you need just a little to bind the potatoes together.

SERVES 4

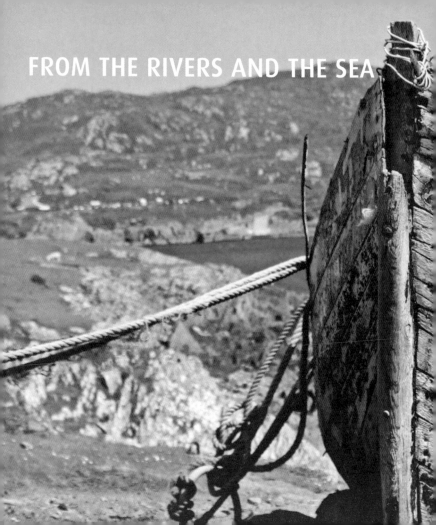

FROM THE RIVERS AND THE SEA

## INGREDIENTS

350 g/12 oz mature
Cheddar cheese,
coarsely grated

100 ml/3½ fl oz
stout

1 tbsp plain flour,
plus extra for dusting

2 tbsp fresh
breadcrumbs

1 tsp mustard
powder

1 egg

1 egg yolk

butter, for greasing

6 x 175-g/6-oz
pieces smoked or
unsmoked haddock

salt and freshly
ground black pepper

lemon slices and
fresh flatleaf parsely,
to garnish

# Baked Haddock with a Cheesy Crust

The secret ingredient in this dish is stout – it really adds flavour to the cheese sauce used to top the fish.

## METHOD

Put the cheese and stout into a saucepan and cook over a low heat until the cheese has melted. Do not bring to the boil.

Add the flour, breadcrumbs and mustard and cook for 5 minutes until the mixture comes away from the sides of the pan. Remove from the heat and leave to cool, then transfer to a food processor or blender and process until smooth. Keep the motor running and slowly add the egg and egg yolk. Transfer to a bowl, cover with clingfilm and chill in the refrigerator for 30 minutes.

Meanwhile, preheat the oven to 180°C/350°F/Gas Mark 4. Place the cheese mixture on a lightly floured work surface and roll out to a thickness of 5 mm/¼ inch.

Grease a baking dish. Place the fish pieces in the dish in a single layer, topping each with a piece of the cheese crust.

Bake in the preheated oven for 10 minutes, or until the fish is cooked through, then place under a hot grill for a few minutes to brown the crust. Garnish with lemon slices and parsley and serve.

SERVES 6

## INGREDIENTS

25 g/1 oz butter

1 small onion, very finely chopped

6 x 175-g/6-oz pieces of cod

1 tsp snipped fresh chives

1 tbsp chopped fresh parsley

300 ml/10 fl oz single cream, plus extra if needed

salt and freshly ground black pepper

### Roux

40 g/1½ oz butter

40 g/1½ oz plain flour

# Cod Baked with Cream

You can use any firm white fish for this quick and easy recipe. It's a good dinner party recipe as it can be cooked ahead of time and reheated before serving.

## METHOD

Heat the butter in a large frying pan over a medium heat until melted. Add the onion and fry, stirring occasionally, until softened and translucent. Do not allow it to brown.

Place the fish in the pan in a single layer and cook for 1 minute on each side. Season with salt and pepper to taste and add the chives and parsley. Add enough cream to cover the fish, reduce the heat and simmer, covered, for 5–10 minutes, until the fish is cooked through.

Meanwhile, make the roux. Heat the butter in a small saucepan until melted, add the flour and cook for at least 2 minutes until the mixture comes away from the sides of the pan. Remove from the heat and set aside until needed.

Use a slotted spoon to transfer the fish to a warmed serving dish. Bring the cooking liquid to the boil, then add the roux and whisk until slightly thickened. Pour over the fish and serve.

**Granny's tip:** If preparing this dish ahead, reheat it in an oven preheated to 180°C/350°F/Gas Mark 4, for up to 30 minutes until the fish is heated through.

SERVES 6

## INGREDIENTS

900 g/2 lb mackerel fillets

55 g/2 oz butter, plus extra for greasing

1 large onion, finely chopped

250 g/9 oz rhubarb, stalks only, finely chopped

handful of fresh white breadcrumbs

salt and freshly ground black pepper

fresh flatleaf parsley sprigs, to garnish

# Rhubarb-stuffed Mackerel

Mackerel is plentiful in Irish coastal waters and it's best cooked as soon as possible after it's caught. Sweet yet tart rhubarb is the perfect complement to this oily fish.

## METHOD

Melt the butter in a heavy-based frying pan over a medium heat, then add the onion and cook until softened and transparent. Add the rhubarb, season with salt and pepper to taste and cook for a further 5 minutes. Stir in the breadcrumbs and remove from the heat.

Meanwhile, preheat the oven to 200°C/400°F/Gas Mark 6 and grease a baking dish. Place the fish fillets on a work surface, skin-side down, and spread the stuffing over them. Roll them up, using a cocktail stick to secure them, if necessary. Bake in the preheated oven for 15–20 minutes.

Divide the cooked mackerel among six warmed plates, garnish with parsley and serve immediately.

SERVES 6

## INGREDIENTS

25 g/1 oz butter
1 tbsp water
2 leeks, thinly sliced
150 ml/5 fl oz single cream
24 shucked oysters, shells reserved
100 g/3½ oz mature Cheddar cheese, coarsely grated
salt and freshly ground black pepper
lemon wedges, to serve

# Oysters with Creamy Leeks & Cheese

Oysters were plentiful and cheap in Ireland and usually eaten cooked rather than raw, baked in the hearth in their shells. This recipe continues that tradition.

## METHOD

Put the butter into a medium-sized saucepan with the water and cook over a medium heat until the butter has melted. Add the leeks and cook for 5 minutes until softened.

Add the cream and continue cooking, stirring constantly, until reduced and thickened slightly. Season to taste with salt and pepper, then remove from the heat.

Place the reserved oyster shells in a grill pan. Divide the creamed leeks among the shells and top each portion with an oyster. Scatter over the cheese and place under a preheated grill for 3–5 minutes until the cheese is golden and bubbling.

Serve immediately with lemon wedges.

**SERVES 6**

## INGREDIENTS

115 g/4 oz butter

4 tsp very finely chopped fresh parsley

½ tsp lemon juice

plain flour, for dusting

6 x 175-g/6-oz fresh mackerel fillets

salt and freshly ground black pepper

# Pan-fried Mackerel with Parsley Butter

**Almost nothing tastes better than mackerel straight from the sea, fried in lots of butter.**

## METHOD

Mix half the butter with the parsley and lemon juice, roll into a cylinder, wrap in greaseproof paper and chill in the refrigerator until hardened.

Season some flour with salt and pepper and use to coat the fish fillets.

Melt the remaining butter in a large frying pan over a medium heat, then add the fish to the pan, skin-side down, and cook for 4–5 minutes. Turn, adding more butter to the pan if necessary, and cook for a further 3 minutes.

Serve immediately on warmed plates, topped with slices of chilled parsley butter.

SERVES 6

## INGREDIENTS

butter, for greasing

2 tbsp chopped fresh dill

125 ml/4 fl oz dry white wine

125 ml/4 fl oz fish stock

1 small carrot, diced

1 celery stick, quartered, leaves retained

1 small onion, finely sliced

1 whole salmon, weighing 2.7 kg/6 lb, cleaned and scaled

lemon slices and chopped fresh herbs, to garnish

mayonnaise, to serve

# Poached Salmon

This is an easy oven method for poaching salmon. When salmon was a once-a-year seasonal treat it was usually cooked whole and served to a crowd.

## METHOD

Grease a large sheet of double thickness kitchen foil and place it in a large roasting tin.

Put all the ingredients except the salmon into a medium-sized saucepan and bring to the boil over a medium heat. Reduce the heat to low and simmer for 20 minutes.

Meanwhile, preheat the oven to 150°C/300°F/Gas Mark 2. Place the salmon on the prepared foil, pour over the liquid and wrap the foil loosely around the fish, sealing the edgings crimping them together with your fingers.

Poach the salmon in the preheated oven for 25–30 minutes, then remove from the oven and leave to sit in the cooking liquid for 30 minutes.

Open the foil and carefully transfer the salmon to a large serving platter. Remove the skin, garnish with lemon slices and fresh herbs and serve warm or cold, with mayonnaise.

**SERVES 15–20**

## INGREDIENTS

55 g/2 oz butter

2 spring onions, finely chopped

650 g/1 lb 7 oz cooked firm white fish, flaked

650 g/1 lb 7 oz cooked mashed potatoes

2 tbsp chopped fresh parsley

3 eggs, beaten

plain flour, for dusting

125 g/4½ oz fresh breadcrumbs

vegetable oil, for shallow-frying

rocket and lemon wedges, to serve

# Fish Cakes

This is another recipe that uses leftover mashed potatoes in a delicious way – although you may be tempted to cook some just so that you can make these tasty fish cakes.

## METHOD

Heat half the butter in a small frying pan until melted. Add the spring onions and cook until softened and translucent.

Put the fish into a mixing bowl with the potatoes, spring onions and the remaining butter, add the parsley and salt and pepper to taste and mix to combine.

Add two-thirds of the eggs and mix, then dust your hands with flour and shape the mixture into four large or six smaller rounds.

Dip the rounds into the remaining beaten egg, then roll them in the breadcrumbs to coat.

Heat enough oil for shallow frying in a large, heavy-based frying pan, then add the rounds and fry for 6–8 minutes on each side until golden brown in colour. Serve immediately on a bed of rocket with lemon wedges for squeezing over.

SERVES 4-6

## INGREDIENTS

100 g/3½ oz raisins

125 g/4½ oz butter, plus extra for greasing

4 x 225-g/8-oz trout, cleaned

1 onion, finely chopped

2 celery sticks, finely chopped

4 spring onions, thinly sliced

100 g/3½ oz toasted flaked almonds

1 tbsp chopped fresh parsley

125 g/4½ oz dried white breadcrumbs

2 eggs, beaten

salt and freshly ground black pepper

# Baked Stuffed Trout

Trout lends itself very well to being baked – the raisins add a little sweetness to the stuffing while keeping the fish moist and succulent.

## METHOD

Preheat the oven to 180°C/350°F/Gas Mark 4 and grease a baking dish large enough to hold the fish in a single layer. Put the raisins into a small bowl, pour over enough hot water to cover, leave to stand for up to 5 minutes, then drain.

Meanwhile, put half the butter into a frying pan and heat until melted, then add the onion, celery and spring onions and cook over a low heat until the vegetables are softened.

Stir in the almonds, raisins and parsley, then remove from the heat and mix in the breadcrumbs with salt and pepper to taste. Add enough of the beaten egg to bind the mixture and gently mix to combine.

Divide the stuffing evenly among the fish, filling the cavities. Dot the fish with the remaining butter, then bake in the preheated oven for 25–30 minutes, basting the fish with the cooking juices from time to time.

**Granny's tip:** If the fish isn't browned at the end of the cooking time, place it under a hot grill for a few seconds.

SERVES 4

## INGREDIENTS

450 g/1 lb mussels, scrubbed and debearded

900 g/2 lb smoked haddock, cooked and flaked

225 g/8 oz cooked peeled prawns

650 g/1 lb 7 oz floury potatoes, peeled and cut into small chunks

70 g/2½ oz butter

25 g/1 oz plain flour

600 ml/1 pint fish stock

350 g/12 oz leeks, thickly sliced

115 g/4 oz button mushrooms, sliced

1 tbsp chopped fresh tarragon

1 tbsp chopped fresh parsley, plus extra sprigs to garnish

salt

**SERVES 4-6**

# Seafood Pie

You can use any white fish in this pie, but the smoked cod adds colour and depth of flavour. For a richer pie, replace a third of the stock with single cream.

## METHOD

Discard any mussels that refuse to close when tapped with a knife. Put the remaining mussels into a large saucepan with 2–3 tablespoons of water. Cover and cook over a high heat for 5 minutes, or until the mussels have opened. Discard any that are still closed, drain and rinse under cold running water and remove the mussels from their shells. Transfer them to a large bowl and add the haddock and prawns.

Cook the potatoes in lightly salted boiling water for 20 minutes, or until tender, then drain and mash well with 25 g/1 oz of the butter.

Meanwhile, melt 25 g/1 oz of the remaining butter in a large saucepan over a medium heat, stir in the flour and cook for 1 minute. Reduce the heat to low, gradually whisk in the stock and cook for 10 minutes until smooth.

Preheat the oven to 180°C/350°F/Gas Mark 4. Melt the remaining butter in a medium-sized saucepan, add the leeks and mushrooms and cook over a medium heat for 5 minutes. Add to the fish and shellfish with the herbs. Pour in the sauce and gently mix together, then transfer the mixture to a large pie dish. Spoon over the mashed potatoes and smooth them with a fork. Cook in the preheated oven for 30–40 minutes, garnish with parsley and serve immediately.

## INGREDIENTS

4 x 225-g/8-oz cod
fillets

1 bay leaf

6 whole black
peppercorns

1 bouquet garni

1 shallot, cut into
quarters

25 g/1 oz butter

25 g/1 oz plain flour

300 ml/10 fl oz milk

2 tbsp finely
chopped fresh
parsley

salt and freshly
ground black pepper

French beans and
lemon wedges, to
serve

# Poached Cod with Parsley Sauce

Cod used to be readily available and
inexpensive and this was a popular Friday
dish. You can use any firm white fish or
even salmon fillets.

## METHOD

Put the cod fillets into a large saucepan with the bay leaf,
peppercorns, bouquet garni, shallot and enough cold water to
cover the fish completely. Bring to the boil over a medium heat,
then reduce the heat to low and simmer for 5 minutes. Remove
from the heat and drain, reserving the cooking liquid. Set the
fish aside and keep warm while you cook the sauce.

Heat the butter in a medium-sized saucepan until melted.
Stir in the flour and cook for 1 minute. Strain the reserved
cooking liquid and gradually add to the flour mixture, whisking
constantly until smooth and thick.

Slowly add the milk, whisking constantly to prevent lumps
forming, and bring to the boil. Reduce the heat to low and cook
for 10 minutes, stirring from time to time. Stir in the parsley
and season to taste with salt and pepper.

Transfer the fish to warmed plates and serve immediately with
French beans and lemon wedges.

SERVES 4

## INGREDIENTS

butter, for greasing

plain flour, for dusting

1 quantity shortcrust pastry (see page 11)

25 g/1 oz dried dulse, soaked in cold water for 10 minutes

300 ml/10 fl oz milk

4 large eggs

100 g/3½ oz mature Cheddar cheese, coarsely grated

salt and freshly ground black pepper

# Seaweed Flan

A seaweed that can be found all along Ireland's western coastline, dulse is high in fibre and rich in vitamins and minerals. It's available dried, and can be reconstituted in cold water.

## METHOD

Preheat the oven to 180°C/350°C/Gas Mark 4. Grease a 23-cm/9-inch flan tin. Roll out the pastry on a lightly floured work surface and use to line the prepared tin.

Drain the dulse, pat it dry and chop it very finely, then sprinkle it evenly in the base of the pastry case.

Put the milk into a bowl, add the eggs and beat well, then add the cheese and stir to combine. Add salt and pepper to taste, then pour the mixture into the pastry case.

Bake in the preheated oven for 20–25 minutes, or until set. Serve warm or cold.

**Granny's tip:** To prevent the egg mixture spilling over on the way to the oven, fill the pastry case two-thirds full, then place in the oven and carefully pour in the remaining mixture.

SERVES 4–6

## INGREDIENTS

2 tbsp olive oil

55 g/2 oz butter

1 shallot, very finely chopped

115 ml/4 fl oz dry white wine or dry cider

4 large scallops

2 egg yolks

2 tbsp cream

55 g/2 oz mature Cheddar cheese, coarsely grated

55 g/2 oz fresh white breadcrumbs

brown soda bread (see page 174), to serve

# Cheesy Scallops

Buy scallops in their half shells, then you can use the shells as serving dishes.

## METHOD

Put the oil and butter into a large frying pan and heat until the butter is melted. Add the shallot and cook over a low heat until softened. Add the wine, increase the heat and bring to the boil.

Remove the scallops from their shells and slice them, reserving the corals. Add to the pan and cook for 1–2 minutes, then add the sliced corals. Cook for a further minute, then remove from the pan with a slotted spoon and divide among the half shells.

Remove the pan from the heat and leave the cooking liquid to cool slightly, then add the egg yolks and stir to combine. Return to a low heat and heat until the sauce thickens, taking care not to allow it to come to the boil.

Add the cream, season to taste with salt and pepper and pour the sauce over the scallops.

Mix the cheese and breadcrumbs together and scatter the mixture over the sauce. Place under a hot grill until the topping begins to brown. Serve immediately with brown soda bread.

SERVES 4

## INGREDIENTS

1 kg/2 lb 4 oz mussels, scrubbed and debearded

150 g/5½ oz butter

4 garlic cloves, crushed

150 g/5½ oz fresh white breadcrumbs

55 g/2 oz mature Cheddar cheese, finely grated

2 tbsp finely chopped fresh flatleaf parsley

# Stuffed Mussels

These are simplicity itself to prepare and make a delicious starter.

## METHOD

Discard any mussels that refuse to close when tapped with a knife. Put the remaining mussels into a large saucepan with 2–3 tablespoons of water. Cover and cook for about 5 minutes, or until all the mussels have opened. Discard any that are still closed, drain and set aside until needed.

Meanwhile, put the butter into a small saucepan and heat over a medium heat until melted. Add the garlic and cook for 1 minute, then stir in the breadcrumbs, cheese and parsley and remove from the heat.

Leaving the mussels in their half shells, arrange them on a baking tray or grill pan in a single layer, top with the breadcrumb mixture and place under a hot grill for 3–5 minutes until the breadcrumbs are golden brown. Serve immediately.

SERVES 4

## INGREDIENTS

4 fresh herrings, filleted
1 onion, sliced into rings
1 tsp salt
1 bay leaf
4 cloves
6 white peppercorns
6 black peppercorns
1 tsp sugar
150 ml/5 fl oz stout
150 ml/5 fl oz white malt vinegar

# Potted Herrings

Stout may seem an unusual ingredient to cook with fish, but the spiced liquid turns into a rich dark jelly when the herrings are chilled overnight.

## METHOD

Preheat the oven to 160°C/325°F/Gas Mark 3. Roll up the herring fillets from the tail end and arrange them, seam underneath, in a casserole dish. Top with the onion rings, salt, bay leaf, peppercorns, cloves and sugar.

Mix the stout and vinegar together and pour the mixture over the fish. Cover and cook in the preheated oven for 50 minutes, then switch off the oven and leave the casserole in it for 2 hours.

Transfer the fish to a serving dish and spoon over some of the cooking liquid. Chill for at least 2 hours, or overnight.

SERVES 4

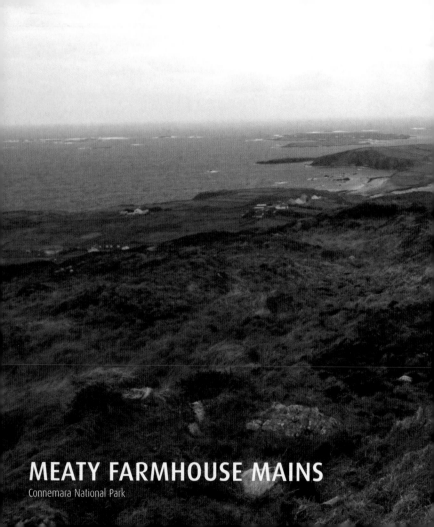

# MEATY FARMHOUSE MAINS

Connemara National Park

## INGREDIENTS

1 loin of pork, weighing about 2.25 kg/5 lb

55 g/2 oz butter

1 onion, finely chopped

100 g/3½ oz fresh white breadcrumbs

2 tbsp chopped mixed herbs, to include parsley, sage and thyme

salt and freshly ground black pepper

roast potatoes and apple sauce, to serve

# Roast Stuffed Loin of Pork

One of the joys of a roast loin of pork is the crackling – you need to give it a good 10 minutes at a high temperature to get it really crisp.

## METHOD

Preheat the oven to 190°C/375°F/Gas Mark 5. Use a very sharp knife to score the skin of the pork at 5-mm/¼-inch intervals along the grain.

Heat the butter in a small frying pan until melted, then add the onions and cook over a low heat for 5 minutes, or until softened and translucent. Remove from the heat, stir in the breadcrumbs, mixed herbs and salt and pepper to taste and leave to cool.

Place the pork on a work surface skin-side down and season with salt and pepper. Spread the stuffing over the pork, then roll up and tie tightly with kitchen string. Generously season the skin with salt, place in a roasting tin and roast in the preheated oven for 2½ hours (or 30 minutes per 450 g/1 lb), basting from time to time.

About 10 minutes before the end of the cooking time increase the oven temperature to 230°C/450°F/Gas Mark 8 and continue cooking until the crackling is crisp and the juices run clear when the thickest part of the meat is pierced with a skewer.

Leave the meat to rest for 10 minutes, then carve and serve with roast potatoes and apple sauce.

**SERVES 6-8**

## INGREDIENTS

25 g/1 oz plain flour, plus extra for dusting

900 g/2 lb rump steak, cubed

85 g/3 oz butter

8 streaky bacon rashers, chopped

5 onions, chopped

1 tbsp raisins

1 tsp soft light brown sugar

300 ml/10 fl oz Irish stout

1 quantity shortcrust pastry (see page 11)

beaten egg, for glazing

salt and freshly ground black pepper

buttered baby carrots (see page 116), to serve

**SERVES 8**

# Beef & Guinness Pie

Beef cooked in dark stout is an unbeatable combination. The long cooking blends all the flavours in a rich and fragrant gravy.

## METHOD

Put the flour into a polythene bag with some salt and pepper. Add the meat, secure the top of the bag and shake until the meat is completely coated in flour.

Melt the butter in a large frying pan, then add the beef and the bacon and cook, stirring occasionally, until browned.

Transfer the meat to a casserole dish. Add the onions to the pan and fry until golden. Add them to the casserole with the raisins, sugar and stout.

Cover tightly, bring to the boil over a medium heat, then reduce the heat and simmer for about 2 hours until the meat is tender, adding more liquid if needed.

Meanwhile, preheat the oven to 200°C/400°F/Gas Mark 6. Transfer the contents of the casserole dish to a deep pie dish.

Roll out the pastry on a lightly floured work surface and use to cover the pie dish, trimming and sealing the edges. Brush with the beaten egg and cook in the preheated oven for 30–35 minutes until golden brown.

Serve hot, with baby carrots.

## INGREDIENTS

3 racks of spring lamb, each with 6 cutlets.

salt and freshly ground pepper

roast potatoes, fresh minted peas (see page 112) and mint jelly (see page 214), to serve

# Roast Rack of Spring Lamb

This is a delicious way to serve spring lamb. The tiny cutlets are a bit fiddly to eat, but cooking on the bone keeps the meat moist and succulent.

## METHOD

Preheat the oven to 220°/425°F/Gas Mark 7. Remove any skin from the racks and score the fat.

Place the racks in a roasting tin, season the meat with salt and pepper and roast, fat side facing upwards, for 25 minutes for rare, or 30 minutes if you prefer them reasonably well done.

Transfer to a warmed serving platter and leave to rest for about 5 minutes before carving.

Serve 3 cutlets per person, with roast potatoes and minted peas, and mint jelly on the side.

**Granny's tip:** Always leave roasts to rest for a few minutes after they come out of the oven so that the juices can be redistributed through the meat.

SERVES 6

## INGREDIENTS

4 gammon steaks
25 g/1 oz butter,
plus extra melted
butter, for brushing
1 small onion, finely
chopped
25 g/1 oz plain flour
175 ml/6 fl oz
water, plus extra if
needed
1 tbsp soft dark
brown sugar
1 tbsp whiskey
salt and freshly
ground black pepper

# Gammon Steaks with Whiskey Sauce

Gammon steaks are very lean and tasty and simple to cook. They're often served garnished with a slice of canned pineapple, but the whiskey sauce in this recipe puts them in a different league.

## METHOD

Brush the steaks on both sides with melted butter, place under a preheated grill and cook for 7–8 minutes on each side.

Meanwhile, heat the butter in a small saucepan until melted. Add the onion and sauté until softened and translucent.

Remove from the heat and stir in the flour to make a thick paste. Return to the heat and slowly add the water, stirring after each addition. Add the sugar, bring to the boil, then reduce the heat and simmer for 2 minutes.

Add the whiskey and season to taste with salt and pepper. If the sauce is too thick add a little more water.

Place the gammon steaks on a warmed serving platter, pour over the sauce and serve immediately.

SERVES 4

## INGREDIENTS

1 kg/2 lb 4 oz
middle neck of lamb,
trimmed and cut into
chunks

4 large potatoes,
peeled and sliced

2 carrots, sliced

2 onions, sliced

500 ml/18 fl oz
water

salt and freshly
ground black pepper

chopped fresh
parsley, to garnish

# Irish Stew

This traditional dish is prepared using economical cuts of lamb that are tenderised slow cooking. It used to be a white stew that included no coloured vegetables – just potatoes and onions or leeks – but today carrots are usually included.

## METHOD

Preheat the oven to 160°C/325°F/Gas Mark 3.

Layer the meat, potatoes, carrots and onions in a casserole dish, adding salt and pepper to each layer and finish with a layer of potatoes.

Add the water, cover with a tight-fitting lid and cook in the preheated oven for at least 2 hours.

Serve in warmed bowls, garnished with parsley.

SERVES 4

## INGREDIENTS

1 tbsp vegetable oil

25 g/1 oz butter

1 chicken, about 1.5 kg/3 lb 5 oz

225 g/8 oz lardons

450 g/1 lb leeks, cut into chunks

250 ml/8 fl oz chicken stock

250 ml/8 fl oz double cream

1 tbsp chopped fresh tarragon

salt and freshly ground black pepper

# Creamy Chicken, Leek & Bacon Casserole

The chicken in this casserole is cooked whole, so it stays succulent and retains all its flavour. The sauce is rich and creamy with a strong hint of tarragon.

## METHOD

Preheat the oven to 180°C/350°F/Gas Mark 4. Heat the oil and butter together in a large casserole dish until the butter is melted. Add the chicken, breast-side down, and cook for 5 minutes until golden. Remove from the casserole dish and set aside.

Add the lardons to the casserole dish and cook for 5 minutes, or until golden. Add the leeks and cook for 5 minutes until they are beginning to brown at the edges. Return the chicken to the casserole, cover and cook in the preheated oven for 1½ hours.

Remove the chicken, bacon and leeks from the casserole with a slotted spoon, set aside and keep warm. Skim the fat from the cooking juices, add the stock and cream to the casserole and bring to the boil over a medium heat. Reduce the heat slightly and cook for 4–5 minutes until the sauce is slightly thickened.

Add the tarragon and salt and pepper to taste. Slice the chicken and serve with the bacon, leeks and the tarragon sauce.

**SERVES 4–6**

## INGREDIENTS

1 rabbit, about
1.25 kg/2 lb 12 oz,
jointed

25 g/1 oz plain flour

25 g/1 oz butter

4 streaky bacon
rashers, roughly
chopped

1 onion, chopped

1 garlic clove,
chopped

450 g/1 lb carrots,
sliced

1 celery stick, sliced

2 white turnips,
chopped

1 bay leaf

1 bouquet garni

500 ml/18 fl oz
chicken stock

salt and freshly
ground black pepper

mashed potatoes, to
serve

# Rabbit Stew

This hearty winter stew is full of colour
and goodness. Ask your butcher to joint
the rabbit if you're not confident about
doing it yourself.

## METHOD

Preheat the oven to 180°C/350°F/Gas Mark 4. Put the rabbit
pieces and flour into a bag with some salt and pepper, secure
the top of the bag and shake well until the meat is completely
coated in flour.

Heat the butter in a large casserole until melted. Add the rabbit
and fry over a medium heat until golden. Remove from the
casserole and set aside.

Add the bacon, onion and garlic to the casserole and
cook, stirring occasionally, until the onion is softened and
transparent. Return the rabbit to the casserole, along with the
remaining vegetables, bay leaf and bouquet garni. Add the
stock, then cover and cook in the preheated oven for 1 hour
and 50 minutes.

Remove the bay leaf and bouquet garni and serve the stew with
mashed potatoes.

**SERVES 4**

## INGREDIENTS

1 young hare, jointed
55 g/2 oz plain flour
85 g butter
300 ml/10 fl oz chicken stock
150 ml/5 fl oz full-bodied red wine
1 onion, peeled and stuck with 8 cloves
1 tsp grated lemon rind
½ tsp ground mace
1 bouquet garni
salt and freshly ground black pepper
carrots and mashed potatoes, to serve

# Jugged Hare

This old-fashioned dish is simply a hare stew – to 'jug' means to stew something in a covered cooking vessel. You could substitute a rabbit for the hare.

## METHOD

Put the hare pieces and flour into a polythene bag with some salt and pepper, secure the top of the bag and shake well until the meat is completely coated in flour.

Heat 55 g/2 oz of the butter in a large saucepan until melted, then add the meat and cook, turning, until browned all over. Remove from the pan, then stir the flour remaining in the polythene bag into the pan juices and cook until beginning to brown. Add the stock and the wine and bring to the boil, stirring constantly.

Add the onion, lemon rind, mace and bouquet garni to the pan, cover and simmer over a low heat for 2–3 hours, until the meat is tender and falling off the bone. Transfer the meat to a warmed serving platter, then strain the sauce, season to taste with salt and pepper and pour over the meat. Serve with carrots and mashed potatoes.

SERVES 4

## INGREDIENTS

450 g/1 lb stewing steak, trimmed and cubed

25 g/1 oz plain flour

1 tbsp vegetable oil

25 g/1 oz butter

1 onion, finely chopped

150 ml/5 fl oz stout

150 ml/5 fl oz beef stock

1 bouquet garni

12 oysters, shucked

plain flour, for dusting

1 quantity shortcrust pastry (see page 11)

1 egg, beaten

salt and freshly ground black pepper

chopped fresh flatleaf parsley, to garnish

**SERVES 4**

# Beef & Oyster Pie

Ingone days oysters were cheap and readily available and were often cooked with beef. This hearty pie includes another traditional and complementary ingredient – stout.

## METHOD

Preheat the oven to 180°C/350°F/Gas Mark 4. Put the beef and flour into a polythene bag with some salt and pepper, secure the top of the bag and shake until the meat is completely coated in flour.

Heat the oil and butter together in a large casserole until the butter is melted. Add the meat and cook for 10 minutes until browned all over. Add the onion and cook for a further 2 minutes, or until just softened.

Add the stout, stock and bouquet garni. Cover and cook in the preheated oven for 1½ hours.

Transfer the contents of the casserole to a pie dish and stir in the oysters. Increase the oven temperature to 200°C/400°F/Gas Mark 6.

Roll out the pastry on a lightly floured work surface and use to cover the pie dish. Trim, crimping the edges, and decorate with cut-out pastry shapes. Brush with beaten egg and bake in the oven for 25 minutes. Serve piping hot, garnished with parsley.

## INGREDIENTS

1 free-range chicken,
about 1.8 kg/4 lb

85 g/3 oz butter

4 streaky bacon
rashers

salt and freshly
ground black pepper

roast potatoes, to
serve

### Stuffing

1 tbsp olive oil

1 onion, finely
chopped

250 g/9 oz fresh
white breadcrumbs

1 tsp chopped fresh
parsley

1 tsp chopped fresh
thyme

# Roast Chicken with Stuffing

Roast chicken was the traditional Sunday
dinner in Irish households. If you use a free-
range bird you'll see why the humble chicken
was worthy of such an important role.

## METHOD

Preheat the oven to 190°C/375°F/Gas Mark 5.

To make the stuffing, heat the oil in a small frying pan, then add the
onion and cook until softened and translucent. Put the breadcrumbs into
a mixing bowl, add the onion and herbs and stir to combine.

Spread the butter all over the top of the chicken and season to taste with
salt and pepper. Stuff the cavity with the stuffing. Lay the bacon rashers
on the breast, overlapping slightly.

Place the chicken in a roasting tin and roast in the preheated oven for 20
minutes per 450 g/1 lb, basting with the cooking juices every 30 minutes.

Remove the bacon after 1 hour. Increase the oven temperature to
220°C/425°F/Gas Mark 7 20 minutes before the end of the cooking time.
Remove the chicken from the oven, transfer to a warmed serving platter
and leave to rest for 20 minutes before serving.

**Granny's tip:** Check whether the chicken is fully cooked inserting
a skewer into the thickest part of the thigh – if the juices run clear, it is
cooked.

**SERVES 6**

## INGREDIENTS

900 g/2 lb stewing steak, cubed
2 tbsp plain flour
vegetable oil, for frying
2 onions, chopped
2 carrots, chopped
2 garlic cloves, chopped
1 swede, chopped
2 celery sticks, chopped
2 tomatoes, peeled, deseeded and chopped
3 potatoes, cut into chunks
1 bouquet garni
750 ml/1¼ pints beef stock
salt and freshly ground black pepper
fresh parsley sprigs, to garnish

### Dumplings

85 g/3 oz self-raising flour
55 g/2 oz fresh white breadcrumbs
15 g/½ oz grated suet
1 tbsp chopped fresh mixed herbs
1 egg, beaten
salt and freshly ground black pepper

**SERVES 6**

# Beef Stew with Dumplings

This is the ultimate winter comfort food, full of hearty flavour. It's a substantial one-pot dish, with no need for extra potatoes or vegetables.

## METHOD

Put the meat and flour into a polythene bag with some salt and pepper, secure the top of the bag and shake until the meat is completely coated in flour.

Heat some oil in a large frying pan, add the beef and cook until browned all over. Remove from the pan and set aside while you fry the onions, carrots, garlic, swede, celery, tomatoes and potatoes.

Place the vegetables in the base of a large casserole dish and put the meat on top. Add the bouquet garni and the stock. Cover and cook over a low heat for 2 hours.

Meanwhile, make the dumplings. Mix all the dry ingredients together in a mixing bowl with salt and pepper to taste, then add the egg to bind the mixture together. Roll the dough into walnut-sized balls, then bring a large saucepan of lightly salted water to the boil, add the dumplings and cook for 15–20 minutes. Drain and add to the stew 20 minutes before the end of the cooking time.

Transfer the stew and dumplings to a serving dish, garnish with parsley and serve.

## INGREDIENTS

1 kg/2 lb 4 oz back bacon in 1 piece

1 head white cabbage, cut into quarters

freshly ground black pepper

knob of butter

boiled potatoes and parsley sauce (see page 70), to serve

# Bacon & Cabbage

Bacon is very salty, so you really do need to boil it off before cooking – and remember not to add any salt to the dish.

## METHOD

Put the bacon into a large saucepan and add cold water to cover. Bring to the boil, drain, then add more cold water to cover, bring to the boil and simmer for 1 hour.

Add the cabbage and simmer for a further 20 minutes.

Remove the bacon from the pan and slice thinly. Drain the cabbage, season with pepper, chop and add the butter.
Serve with the bacon, some boiled potatoes and parsley sauce.

**SERVES 4**

## INGREDIENTS

3 tbsp rapeseed oil

1 onion, chopped,

900 g/2 lb minced cooked lamb

2 carrots, chopped

2 tbsp finely chopped fresh parsley

1 tsp finely chopped fresh thyme

1½ tbsp plain flour

700 ml/1¼ pints lamb or beef stock

900 g/2 lb potatoes, peeled and cut into chunks

125 ml/4 fl oz milk

salt and freshly ground black pepper

# Shepherd's Pie

This is less common than cottage pie, which is made with beef mince, but it is a delicious way of using up the leftover Sunday lamb roast.

## METHOD

Heat 2 tablespoons of the oil in a large frying pan over a medium heat. Add the onion and fry for 5 minutes until translucent. Add the lamb and cook, stirring, for 5 minutes until browned. Add the carrots, parsley and thyme and season with salt and pepper. Cook, stirring, for 2–3 minutes until the carrots are coated in oil.

Stir in the flour, then slowly pour in the stock and bring to the boil, scraping up any sediment from the base of the pan. Reduce the heat to low and simmer for 20–25 minutes until the sauce has thickened.

Meanwhile, preheat the oven to 200°C/400°F/Gas Mark 6. Put the potatoes into a large saucepan of lightly salted water, bring to the boil and cook for 10–12 minutes until tender. Drain and mash well with the milk.

Tip the pie filling into a large baking dish, spread the potato over the filling and bake in the preheated oven for 30 minutes.

**SERVES 4-6**

## INGREDIENTS

vegetable oil, for frying

1 onion, finely chopped

125 g/4 oz streaky bacon rashers, chopped

2 tbsp plain flour

½ tsp dried mixed herbs

450 g/1 lb lamb's liver, cut into bite-sized pieces

225 ml/8 fl oz lamb stock

400 g/14 oz canned chopped tomatoes

1 tbsp Worcestershire sauce

salt and freshly ground black pepper

boiled potatoes and Savoy cabbage (see page 124), to serve

# Lamb's Liver with Bacon

This quick and economical dish is full of flavour and is a favourite winter warmer.

## METHOD

Preheat the oven to 180°C/350°F/Gas Mark 4. Heat the oil in a frying pan, add the onion and bacon and fry until softened. Remove with a slotted spoon, transfer to a casserole dish and set aside.

Mix the flour and dried herbs together in a wide dish and season with salt and pepper.

Toss the liver in the seasoned flour until lightly coated, then add to the pan and fry until lightly browned. Transfer to the casserole dish.

Add the stock to the pan and bring to the boil, then stir in the tomatoes. Add the Worcestershire sauce and bring back to the boil, then remove from the heat and add to the casserole dish.

Cover and cook in the preheated oven for 45 minutes.

Serve with boiled potatoes and Savoy cabbage.

**SERVES 4**

## INGREDIENTS

450 g/1 lb shelled
garden peas
1 tsp sugar
1 fresh mint sprig
25 g/1 oz butter
salt
fresh mint leaves, to
garnish

# Fresh Minted Peas

Adding a little sugar and mint really brings
out the flavour of peas fresh from the
garden. Apart from the salt in the cooking
water they need no other seasoning.

## METHOD

Bring a saucepan of lightly salted water to the boil, add the
peas, sugar and mint sprig, bring back to the boil and cook for
about 4 minutes until the peas are just tender.

Drain, toss with the butter until it has melted and transfer to a
warmed serving dish.

Garnish with mint and serve immediately.

**SERVES 6-8**

## INGREDIENTS

250 g/9 oz carrots,
roughly chopped

450 g/1 lb parsnips,
roughly chopped

55 g/2 oz butter

salt and freshly
ground black pepper

# Parsnip & Carrot Mash

This is a good accompaniment to any roast meat or poultry and any leftovers can be fried up with mashed potatoes.

## METHOD

Bring a large saucepan of lightly salted water to the boil, add the carrots and parsnips, bring back to the boil and cook until soft and tender.

Drain, then add the butter, season to taste with salt and pepper and mash well.

Transfer to a warmed serving dish and serve immediately.

SERVES 6

## INGREDIENTS

450 g/1 lb baby
carrots, trimmed but
unpeeled

55 g/2 oz butter

1 tbsp chopped fresh
parsley

salt and freshly
ground black pepper

# Buttered Baby Carrots

**Nothing beats the taste of the first crop of young carrots. You can also prepare older carrots in this way, but they won't be as sweet and tender as baby carrots.**

## METHOD

Put the whole carrots in a saucepan with enough water to cover them. Bring to the boil, cover and cook over a medium heat for 10 minutes, or until just tender.

Drain, add the butter and leave until it has melted completely. Add the parsley and salt and pepper to taste and toss well. Serve hot.

SERVES 4

## INGREDIENTS

8 leeks, trimmed
and thickly sliced
55 g/2 oz butter
55 g/2 oz plain flour
300 ml/10 fl oz milk
55 g/2 oz mature
Cheddar cheese,
coarsely grated
salt and freshly
ground black pepper.
fresh parsley sprigs,
to garnish

# Leeks Baked with Cheese

Leeks are often used to add flavour to soups and stews but they also make a good accompaniment to many dishes. Cooked in a cheesy sauce, they're a meal in themselves.

## METHOD

Preheat the oven to 200°C/400°F/Gas Mark 6. Bring a saucepan of lightly salted water to the boil, add the leeks and cook for 10 minutes, or until tender. Drain, reserving some of the cooking water.

Heat the butter in a saucepan until melted. Add the flour and cook, stirring, for 1 minute until the mixture comes away from the sides of the pan. Remove from the heat and gradually add the milk and about 150 ml/5 fl oz of the reserved cooking water, stirring constantly to prevent lumps forming.

Return to the heat and bring slowly to the boil, stirring constantly, then simmer for 2 minutes, or until thick. Add the cheese and salt and pepper to taste.

Put half the leeks in the base of a baking dish and cover with half the sauce. Repeat the layers and bake in the preheated oven for 20 minutes until the top is golden. Garnish with parsley and serve hot.

SERVES 4

## INGREDIENTS

700 g/1 lb 9 oz
floury potatoes, cut
into small chunks

125 ml/4 fl oz milk

125 g/4½ oz spring
onions, very finely
sliced

125 g/4½ oz butter

salt and freshly
ground black pepper

# Champ

This delicious recipe comes from
Northern Ireland, where it's a winter
favourite. It's important to serve it with a
pool of melted butter in the middle.

## METHOD

Bring a large saucepan of lightly salted water to the boil, add
the potatoes, bring back to the boil and cook for about 20
minutes until tender. Drain and set aside until needed.

Put the milk into a small saucepan with the spring onions and
bring to the boil. Reduce the heat and simmer for 5 minutes,
or until the spring onions are softened. Remove them with
a slotted spoon, reserving the milk, and beat them into the
potatoes.

Gradually beat the reserved milk into the potatoes until they are
soft and fluffy. Season to taste with salt and pepper, then divide
the potatoes between four warmed dishes, shaping them into a
mound with a slight dip in the middle.

Place a quarter of the butter in each dip and leave it to melt
before serving the champ.

**SERVES 4**

## INGREDIENTS

1 red cabbage

1 cooking apple, peeled, cored and roughly chopped

1 red onion, finely chopped

1 garlic clove, very finely chopped

1 tbsp soft light brown sugar

large pinch of mixed spice

½ tsp ground cloves

½ tsp freshly ground nutmeg

150 ml/5 fl oz red wine vinegar

knob of butter

# Spiced Red Cabbage

The long slow cooking produces a sweet yet spicy result that is the perfect complement to a variety of meat and poultry dishes.

## METHOD

Preheat the oven to 150°C/300°F/Gas Mark 2.

Remove the tough outer leaves of the cabbage, then cut it into quarters and use a sharp knife to cut out the core. Thinly slice the quarters vertically and place in a large casserole dish.

Add the apple, onion, garlic, sugar, mixed spice and cloves and pour over the vinegar. Mix everything together so that all the ingredients are evenly distributed.

Cover tightly and cook in the preheated oven for 2–3 hours, uncovering and stirring occasionally. Add the butter and stir to combine 30 minutes before the end of cooking.

Remove from the oven, transfer to a warmed serving dish and leave to cool a little before serving.

SERVES 6-8

## INGREDIENTS

1 Savoy cabbage
85 g/3 oz butter
salt and freshly
ground black pepper

# Savoy Cabbage Dressed with Butter

The secret to perfectly cooked cabbage is to keep the cooking time short. Over-cooking destroys the flavour, nutrients and texture – and spreads nasty odours throughout the house.

## METHOD

Remove the tough outer leaves of the cabbage and cut it into quarters. Use a sharp knife to cut out the core, then thinly slice the quarters vertically.

Put a little water, 55 g/2 oz of the butter and some salt into a large saucepan and bring to the boil. Add the cabbage and cook, tossing, over a high heat for 1–2 minutes.

Cover the pan and continue to cook for 1–2 minutes. Remove from the heat, add some pepper and the remaining butter and toss to coat.

Transfer to a warmed serving dish and serve immediately.

SERVES 6

## INGREDIENTS

vegetable oil, for greasing

225 g/8 oz minced cooked lamb

1 onion, very finely chopped

1 carrot, very finely chopped

200 g/7 oz canned chopped tomatoes

200 g/7 oz freshly cooked long-grain rice

55 g/2 oz chopped walnuts

2 tbsp dried mixed herbs

200 ml/7 fl oz lamb stock

1 large marrow, halved lengthways and deseeded

55 g/2 oz mature red Cheddar cheese, coarsely grated

salt and freshly ground black pepper

SERVES 6

# Stuffed Marrow

Marrows grow well in Ireland but are often overlooked as a vegetable as they are quite bland. However, they make a good vehicle for a tasty stuffing, topped with golden melted cheese.

## METHOD

Preheat the oven to 200°C/400°F/Gas Mark 6. Grease a large baking dish.

Put the lamb, onion, carrot, tomatoes, rice, walnuts and herbs into a bowl, season to taste with salt and pepper and add enough stock to bind the mixture to a good stuffing consistency.

Put the marrow halves into the prepared dish and fill the cavities with the stuffing. Pour boiling water into the dish to a depth of 1 cm/½ inch. Cover with foil and bake in the preheated oven for 1 hour, or until the marrow is tender.

Remove the foil, scatter the cheese over the filling and bake for a further 15 minutes until the cheese is melted and golden. Serve hot.

## INGREDIENTS

2 heads celery

55 g/2 oz butter

1 onion, thinly sliced

2 bay leaves

100 g/3½ oz fresh white breadcrumbs

55 g/2 oz chopped walnuts

100 ml/3½ fl oz dry white wine

250 ml/9 fl oz vegetable stock

100 ml/3½ fl oz single cream

25 g/1 oz white Cheddar cheese, finely grated

# Creamed Celery Gratin

This is a good accompaniment to roast meat – it also makes a good vegetarian lunch.

## METHOD

Cut the celery sticks into 2.5-cm/1-inch pieces. Melt half the butter in a large frying pan over a medium heat, then add the celery, onion and bay leaves. Season to taste with salt and pepper, then cover and cook for 30–40 minutes, stirring occasionally.

Meanwhile, melt the remaining butter in a separate frying pan, add the breadcrumbs and nuts and cook, stirring frequently until toasted and golden. Remove from the heat and set aside until needed.

Add the wine and stock to the celery, increase the heat to high and cook until the liquid has reduced by two-thirds. Add the cream and cook until the liquid takes on a sauce-like consistency.

Season to taste with salt and pepper, transfer to a baking dish and scatter over the breadcrumb mixture and the cheese. Brown under a medium hot grill for 2 minutes, or until the sauce is bubbling. Remove from the heat and leave to stand for 5–10 minutes before serving.

SERVES 4-6

## INGREDIENTS

6 large tomatoes, halved and deseeded

2 tbsp olive oil, plus extra for drizzling

125 g/4½ oz fresh white breadcrumbs

100 g/3½ oz mature Cheddar cheese, finely grated

1 garlic clove, finely chopped

2 spring onions, finely chopped

2 tbsp chopped fresh parsley

salt and freshly ground black pepper

# Baked Stuffed Tomatoes

This tasty side dish is quick to prepare and cook and is delicious served with grilled meat or fish.

## METHOD

Preheat the oven to 220°C/425°F/Gas Mark 7. Place the tomatoes in a roasting tin, drizzle with oil and season to taste with salt and pepper.

Put the oil, breadcrumbs, cheese, garlic, spring onions and parsley into a bowl and mix to combine.

Fill the tomatoes with the stuffing and bake in the preheated oven for 20 minutes. Drizzle with a little oil and serve immediately.

**SERVES 6**

## INGREDIENTS

6 large salad tomatoes

6 spring onions, white and green parts

2 tbsp chopped fresh parsley

1 tbsp olive oil

1 tsp lemon juice

freshly ground black pepper

# Tomato Salad with Spring Onions

This refreshing salad is prepared with summer vegetables. Add some diced cucumber if you like.

## METHOD

Chop the tomatoes into large chunks. Thinly slice the spring onions and place in a serving bowl with the tomatoes and parsley.

Mix the oil and lemon juice together with pepper to taste, then pour over the salad and toss to coat.

Serve immediately.

**SERVES 4**

## INGREDIENTS

1 butterhead lettuce

100 g/3½ oz cherry tomatoes, halved

6 spring onions, green and white parts, sliced

5-cm/2-inch piece cucumber, cut into small chunks

450 g/1 lb cold boiled baby new potatoes, halved

200 g/7 oz lean cooked ham, cubed

4 tbsp vinaigrette dressing

2 pickled beetroot (see page 218), sliced

6 hardboiled eggs, peeled and quartered lengthways

freshly ground black pepper

# Irish Country Salad

This substantial salad makes the most of seasonal summer vegetables. You could update it with lollo rosso, frisée and pine nuts, but butterhead lettuce is the traditional salad leaf used.

## METHOD

Remove the central core from the lettuce and place the leaves in a large salad bowl.

Add the tomatoes, spring onions, cucumber, potatoes, ham and dressing and gently mix to combine.

Scatter over the beetroot pieces and arrange the egg quarters on top. Season to taste with pepper and serve immediately.

**SERVES 6**

# JUST DESSERTS

## INGREDIENTS

250 g/9 oz plain flour

2 tsp baking powder

1 tsp ground cinnamon

100 g/3½ oz soft light brown sugar

85 g/3 oz butter, melted, plus extra for greasing

150 ml/5 fl oz milk

2 large eggs, beaten

4 Granny Smith apples, cored

250 g/9 oz fresh blackberries

icing sugar, for dusting

# Apple & Blackberry Cake

This deliciously moist dessert cake makes the most of the autumn fruit harvest – apples straight from the orchard and blackberries foraged along country lanes.

## METHOD

Preheat the oven to 190°C/375°F/Gas Mark 5. Grease a 23-cm/9-inch springform cake tin and line the base with baking paper.

Sift the flour, baking powder and cinnamon together into a mixing bowl. Add the sugar, butter, milk and eggs and beat with a hand-held electric mixer until creamy. Pour the batter into the prepared tin.

Cut each apple into eight wedges and arrange the wedges on top of the cake. Add the blackberries, pushing them down into the batter slightly.

Bake in the preheated oven for 45–50 minutes, or until a skewer inserted into the centre of the cake comes out clean. Leave to cool in the tin, then unclip and remove the springform and transfer the cake to a serving plate. Dust with icing sugar just before serving.

**Granny's tip:** Don't use frozen blackberries for this recipe as they will make the cake very soggy.

SERVES 8-10

## INGREDIENTS

6 thin slices day-old white bread, crusts removed

55 g/2 oz butter, plus extra for greasing

55 g/2 oz raisins

55 g/2 oz sultanas

55 g/2 oz caster sugar

2 eggs

300 ml/10 fl oz milk

300 ml/10 fl oz single cream

custard, to serve

# Bread & Butter Pudding

This delicious dessert is very filling, so make sure you leave room for it. For an extra touch of luxury sprinkle over a small glass of brandy before you bake it.

## METHOD

Spread the bread with the butter and cut into triangles. Grease a 1-litre/1¾-pint baking dish and arrange half the bread triangles, buttered side up, in the base. Sprinkle with the raisins, sultanas and half the sugar.

Top with the remaining bread, buttered side up, and sprinkle with the remaining sugar.

Beat the eggs, milk and cream together and pour over the bread. Leave to stand for 30 minutes.

Meanwhile, preheat the oven to 160°C/325°F/Gas Mark 3. Bake the pudding for 45–60 minutes until set and browned on top.

Serve hot, with custard.

SERVES 4

## INGREDIENTS

100 g/3½ oz butter,
softened, plus extra
for greasing

100 g/3½ oz soft
light brown sugar

2 eggs, beaten

1 tsp vanilla extract

100 g/3½ oz self-
raising flour

125 g/4½ oz
thick-cut bitter
marmalade

pouring cream,
to serve

# Steamed Marmalade Pudding

This pudding is the perfect finish to
dinner on a winter's night. You can use
jam instead of marmalade, if you prefer.

## METHOD

Grease a 600-ml/1-pint pudding basin. Cream the butter and
sugar together until pale and fluffy. Gradually beat in the eggs,
then add the vanilla extract and mix to combine.

Sift in the flour and fold it in with a metal spoon.

Put the marmalade into the base of the prepared basin,
then spoon in the batter. Cover the basin with a round of
greaseproof paper, pleated in the middle, and tie on securely
with string.

Place the basin in a saucepan of simmering water and steam for
1½ hours, topping up the pan with boiling water as needed.

Remove the basin from the pan and cut away the paper and
string. Run a knife around the sides of the pudding to release it,
then invert it onto a plate and serve with cream.

**SERVES 4–6**

## INGREDIENTS

butter, for greasing
4 large eggs
25 g/1 oz caster sugar
a few drops of vanilla extract
600 ml/1 pint milk
freshly grated nutmeg, for sprinkling

# Baked Egg Custards

**Although this simple dish can be served with stewed fruit, it is also a delicious dessert in its own right.**

## METHOD

Preheat the oven to 160°C/325°F/Gas Mark 4. Grease four ramekins.

Put the eggs into a large mixing bowl with the sugar and whisk together until creamy. Add a little vanilla extract.

Heat the milk in a saucepan over a medium heat until just coming to the boil. Remove from the heat and gradually pour the milk into the egg mixture, whisking constantly.

Strain the custard through a sieve into the prepared ramekins and grate some nutmeg over each portion.

Put the ramekins into a roasting tin and pour in boiling water until it comes halfway up the sides of the ramekins. Bake in the preheated oven for 45 minutes, or until set but not too firm. Leave to cool slightly and serve warm.

SERVES 4

125 g/4½ oz
pudding rice

600 ml/1 pint milk

400 ml/14 fl oz
sweetened
condensed milk

55 g/2 oz sultanas
(optional)

knob of butter, plus
extra for greasing

whole nutmeg, for
grating

stewed prunes
(optional), to serve

# Rice Pudding

This traditional milk pudding has no
added sugar – it gets all of its sweetness
from the condensed milk and sultanas.

## METHOD

Preheat the oven to 150°C/300°F/Gas Mark 2. Grease a baking
dish.

Put the rice into the prepared dish. Mix the milk and condensed
milk together in a jug and pour the mixture over the rice.

Stir in the sultanas, if using, then dot the butter on top and
grate over a little nutmeg.

Bake in the preheated oven for 30 minutes, then stir and bake
for a further 30 minutes. Stir again, then bake for a further 1
hour until the rice grains have swollen and a golden skin has
formed on top of the pudding.

Grate a little extra nutmeg over each portion and serve hot with
stewed prunes, if using.

**Granny's tip:** Do make sure you use pudding rice as it
releases the starch that gives this pudding its characteristic
sticky consistency.

SERVES 6

## INGREDIENTS

150 ml/5 fl oz water

75 g/2¾ oz sultanas

1 tsp vanilla extract

5 Bramley apples, peeled, cored and sliced

70 g/2½ oz granulated sugar

½ tsp ground cinnamon

½ tsp ground nutmeg

125 g/4½ oz plain flour

100 g/3½ oz soft light brown sugar

85 g/3 oz butter, plus extra for greasing

85 g/3 oz rolled oats

### Whiskey Cream

225 ml/8 fl oz whipping cream

2 tbsp clear honey

2 tbsp whiskey

**SERVES 6**

# Apple Crumble with Whiskey Cream

Apple crumble is one of Ireland's most popular cold weather desserts. The whiskey cream accompaniment elevates the humble crumble to luxury status.

## METHOD

Put the water into a small saucepan and bring to the boil. Add the sultanas and vanilla extract, remove from the heat and leave to stand, covered, for about 1 hour until the liquid has been absorbed the sultanas.

Meanwhile, preheat the oven to 180°C/350°F/Gas Mark 4. Grease a baking dish.

Put the apple slices into a large bowl and toss with the granulated sugar and spices. Stir in the sultanas and any liquid remaining in the pan, and transfer to the prepared baking dish.

Put the flour, brown sugar and butter into a food processor and pulse a few times until coarse crumbs form. Sprinkle the mixture over the fruit and bake in the preheated oven for 40–45 minutes until the apples are soft and the topping is golden.

Meanwhile, prepare the whiskey sauce. Whip the cream until soft peaks hold. Stir the honey into the whiskey to combine, fold into the cream, spoon the mixture over the warm crumble and serve.

**INGREDIENTS**

butter, for greasing

plain flour, for
dusting

1 quantity shortcrust
pastry (see page 11)

450 g/1 lb home-
made strawberry
& vanilla jam (see
page 208)

milk, for brushing

# Jam Tart

This is a great standby dessert and a big
favourite with children. Serve warm with
custard, or cold with whipped cream.

## METHOD

Preheat the oven to 200°C/400°F/Gas Mark 6 and grease a
20-cm/8-inch tart tin.

Roll out the pastry on a floured work surface and use to line the
prepared tin. Chill until needed. Re-roll the pastry trimmings
and cut out 8 strips, each slightly longer than the diameter of
the tin.

Heat the jam over a low heat until warm, then spread it over the
base of pastry case. Weave the pastry strips into a lattice pattern
over the top, pressing the ends into the edge of the pastry case.
Brush the strips and the edge with a little milk and bake in the
preheated oven for about 30 minutes until the pastry is golden.

Leave to cool for at least 30 minutes, then cut into wedges and
serve.

**SERVES 6–8**

## INGREDIENTS

1 quantity shortcrust
pastry (see page 11)

3 eggs

450 g/1 lb cottage
cheese

4 tbsp caster sugar

25 g/1 oz butter,
softened, plus extra
for greasing

finely grated zest
and juice of 1 small
lemon

1 tsp vanilla extract

1 tbsp plain flour,
plus extra for dusting

# Traditional Baked Cheesecake

The traditional Irish baked cheesecake used curd cheese, one of the by-products of cheesemaking. Cottage cheese is an excellent substitute.

## METHOD

Preheat the oven to 180°C/350°F/Gas Mark 4 and grease a 23-cm/9-inch loose-based tart tin. Roll out the pastry on a floured work surface, then use to line the prepared tin.

Separate 2 of the eggs and beat the yolks, then whisk the whites until stiff peaks hold. Put the cheese, 3 tablespoons of the sugar, half the butter and the egg yolks into a bowl and mix to combine.

Stir in the lemon zest and juice and the vanilla extract. Beat well, then gradually fold in the egg whites.

Spread the filling evenly in the pastry case. Beat the remaining egg. Melt the remaining butter in a small saucepan, remove from the heat and mix with the beaten egg, the flour and the remaining sugar. Spread this mixture evenly over the filling.

Bake in the preheated oven for 35–40 minutes, or until golden brown. Leave to cool in the tin, then turn out, cut into wedges and serve.

SERVES 8

## INGREDIENTS

85 g/3 oz sultanas

85 g/3 oz chopped walnuts

25 g/1 oz soft light brown sugar

½ tsp freshly ground nutmeg

100 g/3½ oz butter, softened

6 tart eating apples, such as Granny Smiths, cored

whipped cream or custard, to serve

# Nutty Baked Apples

The apples break down in the oven, so they're really soft and luscious. The nuts provide added texture and flavour.

## METHOD

Preheat the oven to 150°C/300°C/Gas Mark 2.

Put the sultanas and walnuts into a bowl with the sugar, add the nutmeg and stir to combine.

Add the butter and mix well. Spoon the mixture into the holes in the apples, pressing it in well.

Stand the apples in a baking dish, cover with foil and bake in the preheated oven for 35–40 minutes. Remove the foil and cook for a further 20 minutes until the apples are soft.

Transfer to individual serving plates and serve with whipped cream.

SERVES 6

## INGREDIENTS

1 litre unsweetened orange juice

1 tbsp powdered gelatine

200 g/7 oz drained canned mandarin orange segments

mint leaves, to decorate

whipped cream or ice cream, to serve

# Orange Fruit Jellies

Jelly is a favourite children's treat, but it's also a refreshing dessert at the end of a heavy meal. You can use any fruit and fruit juice combination, except pineapple, which interferes with the setting process.

## METHOD

Put half the orange juice into a saucepan and bring to the boil over a medium heat.

Remove from the heat, add the gelatine and whisk until it has dissolved. Add the remaining orange juice and stir well.

Dived the orange segments between six individual moulds, pour over the juice and chill in the refrigerator for 3 hours or until set.

Turn the jellies out of the moulds onto individual plates, decorate with mint leaves and serve with whipped cream.

SERVES 6

## INGREDIENTS

butter, for greasing

8–10 slices day-old white bread, crusts removed

450–600 g/1 lb–1 lb 5 oz mixed summer berries

100 g/3½ oz sugar

pouring cream, to serve

# Summer Pudding

This chilled dessert, which combines the sweet yet tart flavours of summer berries is a great addition to the lunch menu on a lazy summer's day.

## METHOD

Grease a 1.2-litre/2-pint pudding basin. Place a piece of bread in the base, then overlap the remaining slices around the sides, reserving 2 slices for the top.

Put the fruit into a saucepan with the sugar and heat gently until the juices are beginning to run. Remove from the heat.

Pour the fruit mixture into the basin, reserving some of the juice. Cover the top with the reserved bread slices, then place a plate and a weight on top. Chill overnight.

Turn out the pudding onto a serving plate, then pour the reserved juice over, making sure to soak any remaining white patches of bread. Serve with cream.

SERVES 6

## INGREDIENTS

150 ml/5 fl oz white wine

2 tbsp sweet sherry or brandy

juice and finely grated rind of 1 lemon

55 g/2 oz caster sugar

300 ml/10 fl oz double cream

amaretti, to serve

# Syllabub

This luxurious, creamy dessert is deceptive – it tastes refreshing but is strongly laced with alcohol.

## METHOD

Put the wine, sherry and lemon juice and rind into a non-metallic bowl and leave to stand for at least 2 hours. Add the sugar and stir to dissolve.

Pour the cream into a mixing bowl and whip. As soon it begins to thicken, slowly add the wine mixture, whipping constantly until soft peaks hold.

Spoon the syllabub into individual glasses and chill in the refrigerator for at least 1 hour. Serve with amaretti.

SERVES 4

## INGREDIENTS

25 g/1 oz flaked almonds

25 g/1 oz oatmeal

150 ml/ 5 fl oz whipping cream

1½ tbsp clear honey

1 tsp lemon juice

# Flummery

**Deliciously crunchy and creamy, flummery is quick and simple to prepare with basic pantry ingredients and a jug of fresh cream.**

## METHOD

Heat a heavy-based frying pan over a medium heat, add the almonds and oatmeal and stir constantly until they are golden brown, taking care that the almonds don't burn. Remove from the heat, set aside and leave to cool.

Whip the cream until soft peaks hold, then carefully fold in the honey and the lemon juice. Fold in the cold almond and oatmeal mixture, then divide between individual glasses and chill for at least 1 hour before serving.

**Granny's tip:** This is delicious served with seasonal fresh berries or a drizzle of fruit compote.

SERVES 4

## INGREDIENTS

500 g/1 lb 2 oz
rhubarb, stalks only,
chopped into chunks

225 g/8 oz sugar

½ tsp orange extract

500 ml/18 fl oz
whipped cream

# Rhubarb Fool

This deliciously light dessert is perfect in late spring and early summer when rhubarb is in season.

## METHOD

Cook the rhubarb with the sugar and a little water for about 5 minutes until soft. Remove from the heat and set aside some of the rhubarb for topping.

Add the orange extract to the rhubarb, purée with a hand-held blender, then set aside and leave to cool.

Gradually fold the cream into the rhubarb, then spoon into glasses and chill for 20–30 minutes.

Top each portion with some of the reserved rhubarb and serve.

**SERVES 6**

## INGREDIENTS

225 g/ 8 oz Bramley
apples, peeled,
cored and chopped
1 ½ tbsp caster
sugar
1 egg whites
125 ml/4 ½ fl oz
whipped cream
chopped toasted
hazelnuts or flaked
almonds, to decorate

# Apple Snow

This light dessert makes a good ending
to a heavy meal. You could replace the
apples with rhubarb or gooseberries (and
an extra spoon of sugar).

## METHOD

Put the apples and sugar into a saucepan with 1–2 teaspoons
of water and cook over a medium heat until the apples are soft.
Cool the apples.

Whisk the egg whites until soft peaks hold.

Fold the egg whites and cream into the apples, then spoon into
glasses and chill for 20–30 minutes before serving.

Sprinkle with toasted hazelnuts and serve.

SERVES 4

## INGREDIENTS

500 ml/18 fl oz milk

250 ml/9 fl oz double cream

55 g/2 oz dried carrageen moss, washed

1 tsp vanilla extract

100 g/3½ oz caster sugar

mixed berries, to serve

# Carrageen Pudding

Carrageen moss, a type of seaweed, produces a gel when heated. This silky-textured pudding is a good vegetarian alternative to Italian panna cotta.

## METHOD

Put the milk and cream into a saucepan over a medium heat. Add the carrageen moss and stir until it releases a gel.

Add the vanilla extract and sugar and cook, stirring, for a further 5 minutes.

Remove from the heat, strain into ramekins or glasses and chill until set. Top with berries and serve.

SERVES 4

# FROM THE BAKE OVEN

Skerries traditional windmill

## INGREDIENTS

450 g/1 lb plain white flour, plus extra for dusting

1 tsp salt

1 tsp bicarbonate of soda

400 ml/14 fl oz buttermilk

# White Soda Bread

Bread is baked every morning in farmhouse kitchens. With no kneading or proving involved it takes no time at all to rustle up a couple of cakes of soda bread.

## METHOD

Preheat the oven to 230°C/450°F/Gas Mark 8. Dust a baking sheet with flour.

Mix the dry ingredients in a large mixing bowl, then make a well in the centre and gradually add the buttermilk, drawing in the dry ingredients from the sides of the bowl. Mix until a moist dough forms.

Turn out the dough onto a floured work surface and shape it into a round about 5 cm/2 inches high. Place the round on the prepared baking sheet and use a floured knife to cut a deep cross in it.

Bake in the preheated oven for 30–45 minutes until the loaf sounds hollow when tapped on the base.

**MAKES 1 LOAF**

## INGREDIENTS

675 g/1 lb 8 oz
wholemeal flour

450 g/1 lb strong
white flour, plus
extra for dusting

2 tsp bicarbonate
of soda

2 tsp salt

850 ml/1½ pints
buttermilk, plus extra
if needed

# Brown Soda Bread

This is a wholemeal alternative to white
soda bread. White flour is included to
lighten the dough, which would otherwise
be too dense.

## METHOD

Preheat the oven to 230°C/450°F/Gas Mark 8. Dust a large
baking sheet with flour.

Mix the dry ingredients in a large mixing bowl, then make a
well in the centre and gradually add the buttermilk, drawing in
the dry ingredients from the sides of the bowl. Mix until a soft
dough forms, adding more buttermilk if necessary. The dough
should not be too moist.

Turn out the dough onto a floured work surface, divide into
two equal pieces and shape both pieces into a round about
5 cm/2 inches high. Place on the prepared baking sheet and use
a floured knife to cut a deep cross in each round.

Bake in the preheated oven for 15–20 minutes, then reduce
the oven temperature to 200°C/400°F/Gas Mark 6 and bake for
a further 20–25 minutes until the loaves sound hollow when
tapped on the base.

**MAKES 2 LOAVES**

## INGREDIENTS

450 g/1 lb plain white flour, plus extra for dusting

1 tsp salt

1 tsp bicarbonate of soda

125 g/4½ oz currants, raisins or sultanas

400 ml/14 fl oz buttermilk

# Currant Bread

A sweet treat with no added sugar! This is delicious served warm with butter.

## METHOD

Preheat the oven to 230°C/450°F/Gas Mark 8. Dust a baking sheet with flour.

Mix the flour, salt and bicarbonate of soda together in a large mixing bowl, then add the currants and stir until coated in the flour mixture. Make a well in the centre and gradually add the buttermilk, drawing in the dry ingredients from the sides of the bowl. Mix to a wet dough.

Turn out the dough onto a floured work surface and shape it into a round about 5 cm/2 inches in height. Place the round on the prepared baking sheet and use a floured knife to cut a deep cross in it.

Bake in the preheated oven for 30–45 minutes until the loaf sounds hollow when tapped on the base.

**MAKES 1 LOAF**

## INGREDIENTS

butter, for greasing
900 g/2 lb
wholemeal flour
450 g/1 lb plain
white flour
55 g/2 oz caster
sugar
2 tsp salt
3 sachets easy-blend
dried yeast
2 tbsp black treacle
800 ml/1½ pints
lukewarm water

# Treacle Bread

This one-step bread is great for anyone who is a bit wary of baking with yeast – the yeast is added with all the other ingredients, the dough is left to prove in the baking tin and is then put straight into the oven.

## METHOD

Grease a large loaf tin.

Put the wholemeal flour into a bowl and sift in the remaining dry ingredients. Mix the treacle with a little of the water, add to the bowl and mix well to combine.

Put the dough into the prepared tin and leave to stand for about 40 minutes, or until doubled in volume. Meanwhile, preheat the oven to 220°C/425°F/Gas Mark 7.

Put the tin into the preheated oven and immediately reduce the oven temperature to 190°C/375°F/Gas Mark 5. Bake for 1 hour, or until the bread is shrinking from the sides of the tin and sounds hollow when tapped on the base.

Leave to cool in the tin for about 5 minutes, then turn out onto a wire rack and leave to cool completely.

**MAKES 1 LOAF**

## INGREDIENTS

450 g/1 lb self-raising flour, plus extra for dusting

pinch of salt

100 g/3½ oz chilled butter, diced

85 g/3 oz caster sugar

300 ml/10 fl oz buttermilk

milk, for brushing

# Buttermilk Scones

These delicious scones, still warm from the oven, are the perfect after-school snack. With lots of butter and jam, they'll keep the hunger pangs at bay until the evening meal.

## METHOD

Preheat the oven to 220°C/425°F/Gas Mark 7. Dust a baking sheet with flour.

Put the flour, salt and butter into a bowl and rub in with your fingertips until the mixture forms fine crumbs. Add the sugar and mix to combine.

Heat the buttermilk over a low heat until lukewarm. Gradually add to the flour mixture, cutting it in with a knife until just combined. Turn out the dough onto a floured work surface and bring it together with your hands. Use your knuckles to press it out to a thickness of 4 cm/1½ inches, then use a 6-cm/2½-inch round biscuit cutter to cut out 12 rounds, reshaping the trimmings.

Place the scones on the prepared baking sheet, then brush with a little milk and bake in the preheated oven for 10–12 minutes until golden. Remove from the oven and transfer to a wire rack to cool slightly. Serve warm.

**Granny's tip:** Never over-handle scone dough as it makes it dense and heavy. A very light touch is needed for the perfect scone!

**MAKES 12**

## INGREDIENTS

175 g/6 oz
wholemeal flour,
plus extra for dusting

175 g/6 oz plain
flour

½ tsp salt

1 tsp bicarbonate
of soda

55 g/2 oz butter

1 tbsp soft light
brown sugar

200 ml/7 fl oz
buttermilk

1 egg, beaten, for
glazing

# Wheaten Scones

An anytime scone – good with cheese or
soup, or just spread with butter and jam
or marmalade.

## METHOD

Preheat the oven to 200°C/400°F/Gas Mark 6. Dust a baking
sheet with flour.

Put the wholemeal flour, plain flour, salt and bicarbonate of
soda into a bowl and mix to combine. Add the butter and rub
it in with your fingertips until fine crumbs form. Add the sugar
and mix to combine.

Stir in enough buttermilk to make a soft dough. Turn out onto a
floured work surface and knead for about 10 seconds.

Use your knuckles to press out the dough to a thickness of 4
cm/1½ inches, then use a 6-cm/2½-inch round biscuit cutter to
cut out 8–10 rounds, reshaping the trimmings as necessary.

Place the scones on the prepared baking sheet, then brush with
the beaten egg and bake in the preheated oven for 15 minutes,
or until risen and golden. Transfer to a wire rack and leave to
cool slightly. Serve warm.

**MAKES 8-10**

# Coffee & Walnut Cake

This rich cake is an Irish farmhouse classic, usually served at high tea, especially on Sundays.

## METHOD

Preheat the oven to 160°C/325°F/Gas Mark 3. Grease two 20-cm/8-inch sandwich tins and line the bases with baking paper.

Beat the sugar and butter together until light and fluffy. Gradually add the eggs, alternating with two-thirds of the flour. Fold in the baking powder with the remaining flour and the crushed walnuts. Add the coffee extract and fold in carefully.

Divide the batter between the prepared tins and bake in the preheated oven for 30 minutes. Leave to cool in the tins for 10 minutes, then turn out onto a wire rack to cool completely.

Meanwhile, to make the butter cream, cream the butter and sugar together until pale and fluffy. Gradually add the coffee extract, mixing after each addition until incorporated. Chill in the refrigerator until needed.

Spread half the butter cream on the base of one of the cakes and top with the other cake. Spread the remaining butter cream on top, decorate with walnut halves and serve.

## INGREDIENTS

150 g/5½ oz caster sugar

150 g/5½ oz butter, plus extra for greasing

3 eggs, lightly beaten

150 g/5½ oz self-raising flour

1½ tsp baking powder

55 g/2 oz walnuts, crushed into small pieces

4 tbsp coffee extract or cold espresso coffee

10 walnut halves, to decorate

### Butter Cream

100 g/3½ oz butter, softened

225 g/8 oz icing sugar

2 tbsp coffee extract or cold espresso coffee

**SERVES 8**

## INGREDIENTS
225 g/8 oz butter, plus extra for greasing

225 g/8 oz soft light brown sugar

300 ml/10 fl oz stout

225 g/8 oz raisins

225 g/8 oz sultanas

115 g/4 oz chopped mixed peel

450 g/1 lb plain flour

½ tsp bicarbonate of soda

½ tsp allspice

½ tsp ground nutmeg

115 g/4 oz glacé cherries, rinsed, dried and halved

finely grated rind of 1 lemon

3 eggs, beaten

# Porter Cake

This rich fruit cake is made with stout (porter) for extra flavour. It also helps to preserve the cake for longer than a normal fruit cake.

## METHOD

Preheat the oven to 180°C/350°F/Gas Mark 4. Grease a 25-cm/10-inch round cake tin and line with baking paper.

Put the butter, sugar and stout into a saucepan and heat over a low heat until the butter is melted. Add the raisins, sultanas and peel, bring to the boil, then simmer for 10 minutes.

Remove from the heat and leave to cool, then add the flour, bicarbonate of soda, spices, cherries and lemon rind. Gradually add the eggs and mix well to combine.

Pour into the prepared tin and bake in the preheated oven for about 1½ hours until a skewer inserted into the centre comes out clean. Leave to cool in the tin, then cut into wedges to serve.

**SERVES 12**

## INGREDIENTS

175 g/6 oz treacle

55 g/2 oz golden syrup

100 g/3½ oz butter, plus extra for greasing

150 ml/5 fl oz milk

2 eggs, beaten

225 g/8 oz plain flour

55 g/2 oz caster sugar

2 tsp mixed spice

2 tsp ground ginger

1 tsp bicarbonate of soda

# Ginger Cake

Every farmhouse pantry has a few tins of treacle and golden syrup for use in baking. This cut-and-come-again cake makes a great snack or addition to a packed lunch.

## METHOD

Preheat the oven to 150°C/300°F/Gas Mark 2. Grease an 18-cm/7-inch square cake tin and line it with baking paper.

Put the treacle, golden syrup and butter into a saucepan and heat over a medium heat until the butter is melted. Add the milk and the eggs.

Sift the flour, sugar, spices and bicarbonate of soda together into a bowl. Add the treacle mixture and beat until smooth.

Pour the batter into the prepared tin and bake in the preheated oven for 1¼–1½ hours, or until a skewer inserted into the centre of the cake comes out clean.

Leave to cool in the tin for 10 minutes, then turn out onto a wire rack and leave to cool completely. Cut into squares or rectangles and serve.

SERVES 6-8

## INGREDIENTS

225 g/8 oz self-raising flour

pinch of salt

225 g/8 oz glacé cherries, quartered, plus a few whole cherries to decorate

175 g/6 oz butter, plus extra for greasing

175 g/6 oz caster sugar

3 eggs, beaten

4 tbsp milk

¼ tsp vanilla extract

demerara sugar, for sprinkling

# Cherry Cake

Glacé cherries add colour and sweetness to an old-fashioned afternoon tea cake.

## METHOD

Preheat the oven to 180°C/350°F/Gas Mark 4. Grease a 20-cm/8-inch round loose-based cake tin and line the base with baking paper.

Sift the flour and salt into a mixing bowl. Add the cherries and mix until coated with the flour.

Put the butter and caster sugar into a separate bowl and cream together until pale and fluffy. Beat in the eggs, one at a time, adding a little of the flour mixture with each addition. Mix well, then stir in the remaining flour mixture, the milk and vanilla extract and mix until quite stiff.

Put the batter into the prepared tin and level the top. Halve the whole cherries and press them into the top of the cake. Sprinkle with demerara sugar and bake in the preheated oven for 1½ hours until golden and a skewer inserted into the centre comes out clean.

Leave to cool in the tin for 10–15 minutes, then turn out onto a wire rack and leave to cool completely before peeling off the baking paper.

**SERVES 6–8**

## INGREDIENTS

175 g/6 oz butter, softened

175 g/6 oz caster sugar

2 eggs, beaten

150 g/5 ½ oz self-raising flour

25 g/1 oz cocoa power

1 heaped tsp baking powder

85 g/3 oz mashed potatoes

3 tbsp milk

icing sugar, for dusting

# Chocolate Potato Cake

This delicious cake includes potatoes in its list of ingredients. They may seem a strange addition, but they give the cake a very good texture.

## METHOD

Preheat the oven to 190°C/375°F/Gas Mark 5. Grease a 25-cm/10-inch round cake tin and line with baking paper.

Put the butter and caster sugar into a mixing bowl and cream until pale and fluffy. Gradually add the eggs, beating well after each addition.

Sift in the flour, cocoa powder and baking powder and fold in lightly with a metal spoon. Add the mashed potatoes and milk and stir to combine.

Pour the batter into the prepared tin and bake in the preheated oven for 35–40 minutes, or until a skewer inserted into the centre comes out clean.

Leaved to cool in the tin for 10 minutes, then turn out onto a wire rack and leave to cool completely. Dust with icing sugar just before serving.

**SERVES 8-10**

## INGREDIENTS

250 g/9 oz plain flour, plus extra for dusting

2 tsp baking powder

½ tsp salt

200 g/7 oz caster sugar

125 g/4½ oz butter, softened, plus extra for greasing

2 eggs

1 tsp vanilla extract

250 ml/9 fl oz milk

2 tbsp cocoa powder

# Marble Cake

This is more interesting than plain Madeira cake and has a lovely chocolate flavour – fold in the dark batter very gently to keep the colours separate.

## METHOD

Preheat the oven to 180°C/325°F/Gas Mark 4. Grease a 23-cm/9-inch round cake tin and dust with flour, shaking out any excess.

Put all the ingredients except the cocoa powder into a mixing bowl and beat with a hand-held electric mixer until smooth. Pour all but 175 g/6 oz of the batter into the prepared tin.

Stir the cocoa powder into the remaining batter, then drop dessertspoons of it onto the batter in the tin. Use a knife to swirl the two batters together very lightly to get a marbled effect.

Bake in the preheated oven for 30–35 minutes, or until a skewer inserted into the centre comes out clean. Leave to cool in the tin for 10 minutes, then turn out onto a wire rack and leave to cool completely.

MAKES 8–10

## INGREDIENTS

150 g/5½ oz butter, plus extra for greasing

150 g/5½ oz caster sugar

3 eggs, lightly beaten

150 g/5½ oz self-raising flour

1½ tsp baking powder

½ tsp vanilla extract

icing sugar, for dusting

### Filling

4 tbsp home-made raspberry jam

250 ml/9 fl oz double cream, whipped

250 g/9 oz fresh raspberries

# Victoria Sponge

This classic afternoon tea cake is a real farmhouse favourite, sandwiched together with fresh whipped cream, fresh raspberries and home-made raspberry jam.

## METHOD

Preheat the oven to 160°C/325°F/Gas Mark 3. Grease two 20-cm/8-inch sandwich tins and line the bases with baking paper.

Put the butter and sugar into a bowl and cream together until pale and fluffy. Gradually add the eggs, alternating with two-thirds of the flour. Fold in the baking powder with the remaining flour and the vanilla extract.

Divide the batter between the prepared tins and bake in the preheated oven for 30 minutes. Leave to cool in the tins for 10 minutes, then turn out onto a wire rack and leave to cool completely.

To make the filling, spread the jam on the base of one of the cakes. Spread the cream on the jam and scatter over the raspberries, reserving a few for decoration. Place the other cake on top to make a sandwich. Dust with icing sugar, decorate with the reserved raspberries and serve.

SERVES 8

INGREDIENTS

350 g/12 oz rolled oats
175 g/6 oz demerara sugar
pinch of salt
225 g/8 oz butter, plus extra for greasing
2 tbsp golden syrup

# Flapjacks

These chewy yet crunchy fingers will keep in an airtight tin for a week or two.

## METHOD

Preheat the oven to 180°C/325°F/Gas Mark 4. Grease a baking tray.

Put the oats, sugar and salt into a bowl and mix to combine.

Put the butter and golden syrup into a saucepan and heat over a medium heat until the butter is melted.

Pour the butter mixture over the dry ingredients and mix well. Press the mixture into the prepared tray, then bake in the preheated oven for 30 minutes.

Leave to cool in the tray for about 10 minutes, then cut into fingers and transfer to a wire rack to cool completely.

**MAKES ABOUT 24**

# Queen Cakes

These little cakes are traditional for children's parties and are a great addition to a picnic or packed lunch. Children love decorating them, so be prepared for a messy kitchen!

## INGREDIENTS

175 g/6 oz self-raising flour

125 g/4½ oz caster sugar

125 g/4½ oz butter, softened

2 eggs, beaten

2 tbsp cold water

1 tsp vanilla extract

### Icing

200 g/7 oz icing sugar

2 tbsp lukewarm water

liquid food colouring

hundreds and thousands or gold and silver dragées, to decorate

## METHOD

Preheat the oven to 200°C/400°F/Gas Mark 6. Line two 8-hole bun tins with paper cases.

Put the flour, caster sugar, butter, eggs, cold water and vanilla extract into a bowl and beat until smooth. Fill the paper cases two-thirds full with the batter.

Bake in the preheated oven for about 15 minutes until golden, then transfer to a wire tray to cool completely.

To make the icing, sift the icing sugar into a bowl and mix in enough of the lukewarm water to make a thick, smooth paste. Add a few drops of food colouring, then spread the icing over the cakes and sprinkle with hundreds and thousands.

**MAKES 16**

## INGREDIENTS

55 g/2 oz caster sugar

55 g/2 oz butter, softened, plus extra for greasing

1 egg, beaten

½ tsp bicarbonate of soda

½ tsp salt

175 g/6 oz porridge oats

55 g/2 oz raisins or dried cherries

# Sweet Oatcakes

These are quick, simple and delicious – you'll have them in the oven within 10 minutes of assembling your ingredients.

## METHOD

Preheat the oven to 200°C/400°F/Gas Mark 6. Grease a large baking sheet.

Put the sugar and butter into a mixing bowl and cream together until pale and fluffy. Add the egg and mix to combine. Add the bicarbonate of soda, salt, oats and raisins and mix well.

Shape the mixture into 20 walnut-sized balls and place on the prepared baking sheet, spaced well apart to allow for spreading. Bake in the preheated oven for 20 minutes until golden.

Leave to cool on the baking sheet for 10 minutes, then use a spatula to transfer the oatcakes to a wire rack and leave to cool completely.

MAKES 20

## INGREDIENTS

225 g/8 oz
self-raising flour
125 g/4½ oz butter,
plus extra
for greasing
85 g/3 oz caster
sugar
125 g/4½ oz mixed
dried fruit
1 egg, beaten
2 tbsp milk
granulated sugar,
for sprinkling

# Rock Buns

This classic textured bun is great with morning coffee, afternoon tea or as a snack at any time of the day.

## METHOD

Preheat the oven to 200°C/400°F/Gas Mark 6 and grease a large baking tray.

Sift the flour into a mixing bowl, then rub in the butter until fine crumbs form. Add the caster sugar and dried fruit and mix well to combine.

Add the egg and milk and mix to a stiff batter. Drop 12 mounds of the batter onto the prepared tray, spaced well apart to allow for spreading.

Sprinkle the buns with granulated sugar and bake in the preheated oven for 10–15 minutes until golden. Leave to cool in the tin for 5 minutes, then transfer to a wire rack and leave to cool completely.

**MAKES 12**

# PRESERVES

## INGREDIENTS

900 g/2 lb
strawberries, hulled
and halved

3 tbsp lemon juice

400 g/14 oz
preserving sugar

1 tbsp vanilla extract

# Strawberry Jam with Vanilla

This luscious jam has the characteristic loose texture of all home-made strawberry jam. The vanilla adds great depth of flavour.

## METHOD

Put all the ingredients into a large saucepan or preserving pan and bring to the boil over a medium–high heat, stirring frequently.

Reduce the heat and simmer for 1–1½ hours, stirring occasionally and removing any scum that rises to the surface.

Test by putting a teaspoon of the jam onto a cold saucer. If it wrinkles when you push your finger into it, it has reached its setting point.

Pour the jam into sterilised jars, seal tightly and leave to cool before using or storing.

**Granny's tip:** Use preserving sugar if you can get it – it helps with setting.

**MAKES ABOUT
900 KG/2 LB**

## INGREDIENTS

600 g/1 lb 5 oz
blackcurrants,
destalked

500 ml/18 fl oz
water

600 g/1 lb 5 oz
preserving sugar

2 tbsp lemon juice

# Blackcurrant Jam

This is one of the tastiest and most versatile jams you can make – it goes with everything from toast and scones to yogurt and ice cream.

## METHOD

Put the blackcurrants into a large saucepan or preserving pan, add the water and bring to the boil over a medium heat. Reduce the heat to low and simmer for 40 minutes until the liquid has almost evaporated.

Add the sugar and lemon juice, bring back to the boil and cook until the jam has reached its setting point. Test by putting a teaspoon of the jam onto a cold saucer. If it wrinkles when you push your finger into it, it has reached its setting point.

Pour the jam into sterilised jars, seal tightly and leave to cool before using or storing.

**MAKES 900 G/2 LB**

# Green Gooseberry Jam

**This deliciously zingy jam brings the taste of long summer days into the kitchen.**

## INGREDIENTS

1.5 kg/3 lb 5 oz green gooseberries, topped and tailed
500 ml/18 fl oz water
1.5 kg/3 lb 5 oz preserving sugar
juice of 1 lemon

## METHOD

Put the gooseberries into a large saucepan or preserving pan with the water and heat over a medium heat until simmering. Simmer for 30 minutes until the gooseberries are soft and the liquid has reduced about a third.

Add the sugar and lemon juice and heat, stirring, until the sugar has dissolved. Bring to the boil and cook at a rapid boil for 10 minutes until the jam has reached its setting point.

Test by putting a teaspoon of the jam onto a cold saucer. If it wrinkles when you push your finger into it, it has reached its setting point.

Pour the jam into sterilised jars, seal tightly and leave to cool before using or storing.

**MAKES ABOUT 1.5 KG/3 LB 5 OZ**

## INGREDIENTS

600 g/1 lb 5 oz sugar

leaves from a large bunch of mint, finely chopped

225 ml/8 fl oz white wine vinegar

175 ml/6 fl oz water

2 tbsp powdered pectin

# Mint Jelly

This sweet yet tart jelly is the perfect accompaniment to roast lamb. You'll need to use pectin to get the proper consistency.

## METHOD

Put all the ingredients except the pectin into a medium-sized saucepan and bring to the boil over a high heat, stirring to dissolve the sugar. Reduce the heat to low and simmer for about 10 minutes.

Add the pectin and stir to combine, then strain the liquid through a sieve. Pour into sterilised jars, seal tightly and leave to cool before storing or using.

MAKES 2 X 300-G/10½-OZ JARS

# Crab Apple Jelly

Crab apples are hard to come by, although many people grow the trees for their stunning blossoms. The apple is inedible, but produces a deep red jelly, the perfect accompaniment to roast meat or poultry. You will need a jelly bag for this recipe.

## INGREDIENTS

1.8 kg/4 lb crab apples, roughly chopped

1.2 litres/2 pints water

900 g/2 lb preserving sugar

## METHOD

Put the fruit into a large saucepan or preserving pan, add the water and bring to the boil, Reduce the heat and simmer for about 40 minutes until the crab apples are very soft.

Pour the contents of the pan into a jelly bag suspended over a large bowl and leave overnight.

Measure out 1.2 litres/2 pints of the strained juice in the bowl and pour into the pan. Add the sugar and heat, stirring, over a low heat until the sugar has dissolved, then increase the heat to high, bring to the boil and boil rapidly until the liquid reaches setting point. Test by putting a teaspoon of the jam onto a cold saucer. If it wrinkles when you push your finger into it, it has reached its setting point.

Remove any scum from the top of the jelly, pour into sterilised jars and seal tightly. Leave to cool until ready to use or store.

**MAKES ABOUT 1.8 KG/4 LB**

**Granny's tip:** Never press liquid through a jelly bag – particles of the fruit will break down and make the jelly cloudy. Just leave it alone and time will do the work.

## INGREDIENTS

1.3 kg/3 lb small beetroot, unpeeled

1 tsp salt

600 ml/1 pint malt vinegar

1 tbsp whole black peppercorns

1 tbsp allspice berries

# Pickled Beetroot

Beetroot has always been popular in Ireland – in season it was often made into a savoury jelly and served with cold meat. However, most of the crop was pickled for use throughout the year.

## METHOD

Put the beetroot into a large saucepan with the salt and add water to cover. Bring to the boil over a low heat, then simmer for about 2 hours until tender. Remove from the pan with a slotted spoon and leave to cool.

Meanwhile, put the vinegar into a saucepan with the peppercorns and allspice, bring to the boil and boil for 10 minutes. Remove from the heat and leave to cool.

Peel the cooled beetroot, then slice thickly and pile into sterilised Kilner jars. Pour over the cooled vinegar and spice mixture and seal tightly.

**Granny's tip:** Don't peel the beetroot before cooking as they will disintegrate in the cooking water.

MAKES 1.3 KG/3 LB

## INGREDIENTS

2.5 kg/5 lb 8 oz
green tomatoes,
peeled

500 g/1 lb 2 oz
onions, finely
chopped

1 tbsp salt

500 g/1 lb 2 oz soft
dark brown sugar

1.2 litres/2 pints
malt vinegar

500 g/1 lb 2 oz
Bramley apples,
peeled, cored and
finely chopped

500 g/1 lb 2 oz
sultanas, finely
chopped

1 tbsp pickling spices

# Green Tomato Chutney

At the end of the summer there are
always those tomatoes that stubbornly
refuse to ripen. This chutney is a great
way to use them up and is the perfect
accompaniment to cheese and cold meat.

## METHOD

Put the tomatoes and onions into a bowl with the salt, cover
and leave overnight.

The next day, put the sugar and vinegar into a large saucepan
and bring to the boil, stirring constantly to dissolve the sugar.
Add the apples and sultanas and simmer for about 10 minutes.

Strain the tomatoes and onions (do not rinse, you need the
salt), add to the pan and bring back to the boil.

Simmer for at least 1 hour, stirring occasionally, until the
chutney is thick. Transfer to sterilised jars and seal tightly until
ready to use.

**MAKES ABOUT 3 KG/6 LB 8 OZ**

## INGREDIENTS

225 g/8 oz white onions, grated

1.6 kg/3 lb 8 oz ripe tomatoes, chopped

300 ml/10 fl oz malt vinegar

100 g/3½ oz caster sugar

1 tsp salt

1 tsp whole black peppercorns

1 tsp cloves

1 tsp allspice berries

# Tomato Ketchup

This home-made version of the popular condiment makes commercial varieties pale into insignificance. It's a good way to use up a glut of tomatoes.

## METHOD

Put the onions, tomatoes and vinegar into a large saucepan or preserving pan and bring to the boil over a medium heat. Reduce the heat to low and simmer until the tomatoes are softened.

Pass the mixture through a non-metallic sieve and return the sieved pulp to the pan with the sugar and salt. Put the peppercorns, cloves and allspice berries into a square of muslin and tie the corners together to secure. Drop the spice bag into the pan, bring the pulp to the boil over a low heat and simmer for about 30 minutes.

Remove the spice bag and pour the ketchup into sterilised bottles or jars. Seal tightly and leave to cool before using or storing.

**MAKES ABOUT 1.2 LITRES/2 PINTS**

FROM THE STILLROOM

## INGREDIENTS

4.8-litre/8-pint
bucket of dandelion
petals

4.8 litres/8 pints
boiling water

1.5 kg/3 lb 5 oz
sugar

grated zest and juice
of 4 large lemons

200 ml/7 fl oz
white grape juice
concentrate

1 sachet white wine
yeast

pinch of yeast
nutrient

# Dandelion Wine

This lovely sweet white wine has quite a
long fermentation period, but the results
are worth the wait.

## METHOD

Pour the water over the dandelion petals, cover and leave to
stand for 2 days, stirring occasionally.

Pour the dandelion mixture into a large saucepan, add the
lemon zest and bring to the boil. Add the sugar, stirring until it
has dissolved, and boil vigorously for 5 minutes.

Remove from the heat, add the lemon juice and grape juice
concentrate and stir.

Sterilise the dandelion bucket using a campden tablet (available
from most pharmacies), then pour in the dandelion mixture,
cover and leave to cool. Add the yeast and yeast nutrient, cover
and leave to ferment for three days.

Pour the liquid through a sieve and funnel into a demijohn
fitted with a bubble trap. Leave to ferment for up to two
months, then decant into a clean demijohn and bottle when the
sediment has sunk to the bottom.

**Granny's tip:** Don't include any of the green dandelion
flowerheads, as these will give a bitter taste to the wine.

**MAKES ABOUT 6 LITRES/10½ PINTS**

## INGREDIENTS

350 g/12 oz sugar

450 g/1 lb fresh or frozen blackberries

500 ml/18 fl oz vodka

500 ml/18 fl oz brandy

grated rind of 2 lemons

# Blackberry Brandy

This is a lovely winter liqueur – if you make it when the blackberries are in season it will be ready to drink at Christmas.

## METHOD

Divide the sugar and blackberries between two large Kilner jars. Divide the vodka and brandy between the jars, seal and shake to combine the ingredients.

Place in a dark place and shake once a week.

After 10 weeks, strain the brandy through a muslin-lined non-metallic sieve into bottles and seal until needed.

**MAKES ABOUT 2 LITRES/3½ PINTS**

## INGREDIENTS

500 g/1 lb 2 oz
sloes, picked over

250 g/9 oz sugar

1 litre/1¾ pints gin

# Sloe Gin

This gin has a lovely deep red colour and is often used in cocktails, although it's also delicious neat. It's ready to drink after 2 months, but it will improve with age.

## METHOD

Prick the sloes with a cocktail stick and divide between two 1-litre/¾-pint Kilner jars.

Add the sugar and gin and seal. Shake well every day for a week, then leave the jars in a cool place for at least 2 months.

Line a non-metallic sieve with muslin and strain the gin through it.

Decant into sterilised bottles and seal. It's ready to drink once it's bottled, but the flavour will improve over time.

**MAKES 1 LITRE/1¾ PINTS**

## INGREDIENTS

zest and juice of
6 large unwaxed
lemons

150 g/5½ oz sugar,
plus extra if needed

1.5 litres/2½ pints
boiling water

# Lemonade

This is the most refreshing thing you can drink on a warm summer's day, served with ice and diluted with sparkling water.

## METHOD

Put the lemon zest and juice into a large bowl. Add the sugar and water, cover and leave to stand in a cool place for at least 8 hours.

Stir again and add more sugar if needed. Strain through a coarse, non-metallic sieve, making sure some of the lemon 'bits' get through.

Decant into sterilised bottles, seal and chill. The lemonade can be served neat, but is more refreshing when diluted with ice-cold water.

**MAKES ABOUT 1.5 LITRES/2½ PINTS**

## INGREDIENTS

115 g/4 oz pearl barley, well rinsed

grated zest and juice of 6 large unwaxed lemons

150 g/5½ oz sugar, plus extra if needed

1.5 litres/2¾ pints boiling water

# Lemon Barley Water

This refreshingly tangy drink is said to have great kidney-cleansing properties and was often served to invalids.

## METHOD

Put the barley into a small saucepan and just cover with water. Bring to the boil over a medium heat, then reduce the heat and simmer for up to 5 minutes. Drain, rinse and drain again.

Put the lemon zest and juice into a large bowl. Add the sugar, water and barley, cover and leave to stand in a cool place for at least 24 hours.

Stir again and add more sugar if needed. Strain through a non-metallic sieve, decant into sterilised bottles and seal tightly. Serve diluted with chilled water.

**MAKES 1.5–2 LITRES/2¾–3½ PINTS**

## INGREDIENTS

2 unwaxed lemons
2.5 kg/5 lb 8 oz sugar
1.5 litres/2¾ pints water
20 fresh elderflower heads, washed
85 g/3 oz citric acid

# Elderflower Cordial

This is a deliciously refreshing citrussy drink. Dilute it with sparkling water or mix it with tonic water and a dash of angostura bitters.

## METHOD

Zest the lemons and slice them into rounds.

Put the sugar and water into a large saucepan and heat over a low heat, stirring occasionally, until the sugar has dissolved. Bring to the boil, then remove from the heat.

Add the elderflowers, lemon zest and lemon slices to the syrup along with the citric acid. Stir well to combine, then cover and leave in a cool place for 24 hours.

Line a non-metallic sieve with muslin and use to strain the cordial. Decant into sterilised bottles and seal tightly. Serve diluted with water.

**Granny's tip:** The cordial will keep in the refrigerator for up to six weeks.

MAKES ABOUT 1.5 LITRES/2¾ PINTS

# LET'S CELEBRATE!

Winter in the Wicklow mountains

## INGREDIENTS

ham joint on the bone,
about 5 kg/11 lb 4 oz
85 g/3 oz soft dark
brown sugar
85 g/3 oz wholegrain
mustard
handful of cloves

# Traditional Christmas Baked Ham

This is usually served with the turkey or goose on Christmas Day, but there are usually a lot of leftovers, which can be eaten cold the following day, with chutney, pickles and brown soda bread.

## METHOD

Soak the ham overnight in enough cold water to cover it completely, changing the water at least twice.

Preheat the oven to 180°C/350°F/Gas Mark 4. Drain the ham, wrap it tightly in kitchen foil and place in a large roasting tin. Bake in the preheated oven for 3 hours.

Remove the ham from the oven and increase the heat to 200°C/400°F/Gas Mark 6. Use a sharp knife to remove the rind from the ham, leaving a good layer of fat. Score the fat in a diamond-shaped pattern.

Mix the sugar and mustard together and rub all over the ham. Stud each diamond with a clove, return to the oven and bake, uncovered, for 30 minutes until the crust is sticky and the ham is cooked through.

**SERVES 12**

## INGREDIENTS

225 g/8 oz salt
1.25 kg/2 lb 12 oz
silverside of beef,
boned and unrolled
55 g/2 oz soft light
brown sugar
½ tsp each ground
allspice, ground
cloves, grated
nutmeg
1 bay leaf, crumbled
1 tbsp saltpetre
55 g/2 oz treacle
2 carrots, cut into
chunks
1 onion, roughly
chopped
freshly ground black
pepper

# Spiced Beef

This is prepared in advance and is useful for all those occasions over Christmas when unexpected visitors call. The spices preserve the beef and it can be served at a moment's notice with crusty bread, gherkins, chutney, pickled beetroot or other garnishes.

## METHOD

Rub the salt into the beef and leave in a cool place for at least 8 hours, then wipe the beef with kitchen paper to remove the salt.

Put the sugar, spices, bay leaf, saltpetre and some pepper into a bowl and mix to combine.

Sprinkle the spice mixture over the beef and leave in a cool place for 8 hours.

Heat the treacle in a small saucepan and pour it over the beef. Turn the beef in its marinade once a day for a week.

To cook the beef, roll it up and tie it with string. Bring a large saucepan of water to the boil. Add the carrots, onion and beef. Bring back to the boil, then reduce the heat, cover and simmer for 3–4 hours. Remove from the heat and leave to cool in the cooking liquid.

Drain the liquid, then place a weighted plate on top of the beef and leave to stand for 8 hours. Slice thinly to serve.

**SERVES 8**

## INGREDIENTS

1 half leg of lamb, fillet end, about 2 kg/4 lb 8 oz
2 garlic cloves, peeled and sliced
leaves of 1 large fresh rosemary sprig
salt and freshly ground black pepper
mint jelly (see page 214), to serve

### Gravy

2 tbsp plain flour
125 ml/4 fl oz lamb or beef stock
125 ml/4 fl oz red wine

# Roast Leg of Spring Lamb

This delicious joint, cooked in red wine and infused with garlic and rosemary, is a more modern take on the traditional Easter Sunday lunch main course.

## METHOD

Preheat the oven to 230°C/450°F/Gas Mark 8. Put the lamb on a rack in a deep roasting tin. Using a sharp knife, make slits in the skin about 1 cm/½ inch deep.

Rub salt and pepper all over the skin, then insert the garlic slices and rosemary leaves into the slits.

Roast in the preheated oven for 30 minutes, then reduce the heat to 180°C/350°F/Gas Mark 4 and roast for a further 30 minutes per 450 g/1 lb. Remove from the oven and leave to rest for 20 minutes.

Meanwhile, to make the gravy, pour off most of the fat from the tin, then sprinkle the flour over the remaining sediment. Whisk over a medium heat until smooth, then gradually whisk in the stock and wine. Bring to the boil and bubble until reduced and thickened.

Carve the lamb into slices and serve on warmed plates with the gravy and some mint jelly.

**SERVES 6**

## INGREDIENTS

175 g/6 oz butter, plus extra for greasing

175 g/6 oz caster sugar

3 large eggs, beaten

350 g/12 oz mixed currants and sultanas

55 g/2 oz chopped mixed peel

grated zest of 1 orange

grated zest of 1 lemon

225 g/8 oz self-raising flour

1 tsp ground mixed spice

3 tbsp brandy

### Topping

450 g/1 lb marzipan

2 tsp apricot jam

1 egg, beaten

**SERVES 10**

# Simnel Cake

Simnel cakes were made by servant girls using ingredients supplied by their employers and were given to their mothers on Mothering Sunday. The cake has become a modern Easter tradition.

## METHOD

Preheat the oven to 150°C/300°F/Gas Mark 2. Grease a 20-cm/8-inch round cake tin and line with baking paper.

Put the butter and sugar into a mixing bowl and cream together until pale and fluffy. Gradually add the eggs, beating well after each addition. Fold in the mixed dried fruit, peel, orange zest and lemon zest.

Sift in the flour and mixed spice and, using a metal spoon, fold in very carefully with the brandy. Spoon the batter into the prepared tin and level the top. Bake in the preheated oven for 2½–3 hours. Leave to cool in the tin for 15 minutes, then turn out onto a wire rack and leave to cool completely. Remove the baking paper.

Meanwhile, make the topping. Roll out the marzipan and cut into a 20-cm/8-inch round. Roll the trimmings into balls. Brush the top of the cake with the jam and place the marzipan round on top. Decorate with the marzipan balls. Brush with beaten egg and grill under a medium grill until toasted.

## INGREDIENTS

175 g/6 oz butter, softened, plus extra for greasing

175 g/6 oz caster sugar

1 egg, beaten

1 tbsp milk

55 g/2 oz chopped mixed peel

115 g/4 oz currants or dried cherries

350 g/12 oz plain flour, plus extra for dusting

1 tsp ground mixed spice

### Glaze

1 egg white, beaten

2 tbsp caster sugar

# Easter Biscuits

These light little biscuits contain many of the ingredients that were forbidden during the strict Lenten season.

## METHOD

Preheat the oven to 180°C/350°F/Gas Mark 4. Grease two large baking sheets. Put the butter and sugar into a mixing bowl and cream together until pale and fluffy. Gradually beat in the egg and milk, then stir in the peel and currants.

Sift in the flour and mixed spice and mix to a firm dough. Knead until smooth, then turn out onto a floured work surface and roll out to a thickness of 5 mm/¼ inch. Cut out 24 rounds with a 5-cm/2-inch round cutter, rerolling and using the trimmings. Place the rounds on the prepared baking sheets and bake in the preheated oven for 10 minutes.

Remove from the oven – do not switch off the oven – and brush with the egg white. Sprinkle with sugar and return to the oven for 5 minutes. Leave to cool on the baking sheets for 2 minutes, then transfer to wire racks and leave to cool completely.

**MAKES 24**

## INGREDIENTS

butter, for greasing
1 large Savoy cabbage, outer leaves discarded
125 g/4½ oz white bread slices
450 g/1 lb fresh beef or lamb mince
1 small onion, finely chopped
1 egg, beaten
salt and freshly ground black pepper

### Tomato Sauce

1 tbsp olive oil
1 small onion, very finely chopped
1 garlic clove, very finely chopped
4 large tomatoes, peeled and chopped
salt and freshly ground black pepper

**SERVES 4**

# Stuffed Cabbage with Tomato Sauce

Stuffed cabbage rolls are a traditional Halloween dish, but this layered pudding is less fiddly to prepare.

## METHOD

Grease a 1-litre/1¾-pint pudding basin and a square of greaseproof paper. Take the leaves off the cabbage, add to a saucepan of salted boiling water and cook for 5 minutes. Drain.

Soak the bread slices in a little water for 3 minutes, then squeeze dry and place in a mixing bowl. Add the meat and mix well, then add the onion, season to taste with salt and pepper and mix in the egg so that mixture binds together.

Starting and finishing with cabbage, layer the meat and cabbage in the basin. Cover with the greaseproof paper and a square of kitchen foil, tying them in place with kitchen string. Place in a large saucepan of simmering water and steam for 1½ hours.

Meanwhile, make the tomato sauce. Heat the oil in a heavy-based frying pan, add the onion and garlic and cook over a low heat, stirring occasionally, until the onion is softened and translucent. Add the tomatoes with salt and pepper to taste and cook for a further 10 minutes, or until they have broken down and the sauce is bubbling gently. Add a little water if it's too thick.

Turn out the stuffed cabbage onto a warmed serving platter, slice and serve with the tomato sauce.

## INGREDIENTS

55 g/2 oz butter

125 g/4½ oz onions, finely chopped

450 g/1 lb cold mashed potatoes

4 tbsp milk

225 g/8 oz cold cooked cabbage

salt and freshly ground black pepper

# Colcannon

Delicious at any time of year, this is traditionally served at Halloween. It's a great way of using up leftover potatoes and cabbage.

## METHOD

Melt the butter in a large frying pan over a medium heat, then add the onion and cook until softened.

Add the potatoes and milk to the pan and season with salt and pepper to taste, then stir until heated through.

Add the cabbage and beat into the potato mixture until the mixture is pale green in colour and has a fluffy texture. As soon as it is heated through it's ready to serve.

**SERVES 4**

## INGREDIENTS

450 g/1 lb plain flour

½ tsp freshly grated nutmeg

pinch of salt

15 g/½ oz fresh yeast

55 g/2 oz soft light brown sugar

300 ml/10 fl oz lukewarm milk

2 eggs, beaten

55 g/2 oz butter, plus extra for greasing

115 g/4 oz chopped mixed peel

225 g/8 oz currants

225 g/8 oz raisins

1 egg yolk, beaten, for glazing

# Barm Brack

## This traditional Halloween treat is delicious served warm with lots of butter.

### METHOD

Grease a 20-cm/8-inch round cake tin. Sift the flour, nutmeg and salt into a large mixing bowl.

In a separate bowl, blend the yeast with 1 teaspoon of the sugar and a little of the milk until it froths.

Add the remaining sugar to the flour mixture. Add the remaining milk to the yeast mixture, then add to the flour with the eggs and butter. Mix with a wooden spoon for about 10 minutes until stiff.

Fold in the dried fruit, then transfer the batter to the prepared tin. Cover with a damp tea towel and leave to rise for about 1 hour until doubled in size.

Meanwhile, preheat the oven to 200°C/400°F/Gas Mark 6. Bake the brack in the preheated oven for 1 hour, then glaze with the beaten egg yolk and bake for a further 5 minutes.

**SERVES 10–12**

*For permission to reproduce copyright photographs, the publisher gratefully acknowledges the following:*

p1 Shutterstock / A. Sokol
p3 Shutterstock / R. Semik
p7 Shutterstock / A. Sokol
p11 Shutterstock / Prostock
p12 Shutterstock / Swirling Vortex
p15 Shutterstock / A. Chavdar
p17 Shutterstock / Aigneis
p19 Kippers / SteveWoods
p21 Ben Potter
p23 Shutterstock / Gayane
p24 Shutterstock / aaabbbccc
p26 Shutterstock / AS Food studio
p29 Shutterstock / Elena Veselova
p31 Ben Potter
p33 Shutterstock / J. Beug
p35 Ben Potter
p37 Ben Potter
p39 Ben Potter
p41 Ben Potter
p43 Ben Potter
p45 Ben Potter
p47 Ben Potter
p49 Ben Potter
p50 Shutterstock / Swirling Vortex
p53 Ben Potter
p55 Ben Potter
p57 Ben Potter
p59 Ben Potter
p61 Ben Potter
p63 Ben Potter
p65 Ben Potter
p67 Ben Potter
p69 Shutterstock / Maria Kovaleva
p71 Shutterstock / Robin Stewart
p73 Ben Potter
p75 Shutterstock / Arayaeng
p77 Shutterstock / Zhan Gasparyan
p79 Ben Potter

p80 Shutterstock / Ash
p83 Tony Potter
p85 Ben Potter
p87 Shutterstock / Maksim Toome
p89 Shutterstock / Alison Ashwort
p91 Shutterstock / CKP
p93 Ben Potter
p95 Shutterstock / Fanfo
p97 Shutterstock / Jacques Palut
p99 Ben Potter
p101 Shutterstock / Antony Lynn-Hill
p103 Shutterstock / Elena Mayne
p105 Ben Potter
p107 Shutterstock / Farbled
p109 Ben Potter
p110 Shutterstock / Maria Janus
p113 Shutterstock / Ziashusha
p115 Shutterstock / Brighton
p117 Shutterstock / Africa Studio
p119 Shutterstock / Ahanov Michael
p121 Shutterstock / Joerg Beuge
p123 Shutterstock / Maria Kovaleva
p125 Ben Potter
p127 Shutterstock / Gayvoronskaya Yana
p129 Shutterstock / vsl
p131 Shutterstock / Tmalucelli
p133 Shutterstock / Lucie Peclova
p135 Ben Potter
p136 Shutterstock / Alexander Narraina
p139 Shutterstock / Bartosz Luczak
p141 Shutterstock / Monkey Business

p143 Ben Potter
p145 Shutterstock / Studio Barcelona
p147 Shutterstock / Anamaria Mejia
p149 Shutterstock / Anikona Ann
p151 Shutterstock / Canbedone
p153 Shutterstock / Olesya Baron
p155 Shutterstock / Africa Studio
p157 Shutterstock / Alisa Farov
p159 Shutterstock / Maria Medvedeva
p161 Shutterstock / Jack Cobben
p163 Ben Potter
p165 Shutterstock / Monkey Business Images
p167 Ben Potter
p169 Shutterstock / Liliia Bielopolska
p170 Shutterstock / Aitormmfoto
p173 Shutterstock / Laura Adamache
p175 Shutterstock / Alp Aksoy
p177 Shutterstock / An Nguyen
p179 Shutterstock / Galina Bahlyk
p181 Shutterstock / Maria Kovaleva
p183 Shutterstock / Joerg Beuge
p185 Shutterstock / Magdanatka
p187 Shutterstock / CKP
p189 Glen Wilkins / Alamy Stock
p191 Ben Potter
p193 Shutterstock / Margouillat

p195 Shutterstock /Successful Model
p197 Shutterstock / Roxanne Cooke
p199 Shutterstock / CKP
p201 Shutterstock / Kitch Bain
p203 Shutterstock / Dmytro Ostapenko
p205 Shutterstock / D. Pimborough
p207 Shutterstock / Joerg Beuge
p209 Shutterstock / Alter-ego
p211 Shutterstock / Almaje
p213 Ben Potter
p215 Shutterstock / Monkey Business Images
p217 Shutterstock / CKP
p219 Shutterstock / riggsby
p221 Shutterstock / Hans Geel
p223 Shutterstock / Bjoern Wylezichb
p224 Shutterstock / C Tatiana
p227 Shutterstock / Smile
p229 Shutterstock / Handmade Pictures
p231 Ben Potter
p233 Shutterstock / JeniFoto
p235 Shutterstock / Kate Grigoryeva
p237 Shutterstock / Bildagentur Zoonar GmbH
p239 Shutterstock / Riganmc
p241 Shutterstock / Bartosz Luczak
p243 Tony Potter
p245 Shutterstock / Lesya Dolyuk
p247 Shutterstock / Annaustynnikova
p249 Ben Potter
p251 Shutterstock / Slawomir Fajer
p253 Shutterstock / Fanfo
p255 Shutterstock / Monkey Business Images